SIMPLE-TO-SEW

SLIPCOVERS
&
COVER-UPS

Simple-to-Sew
SLIPCOVERS
&
COVER-UPS

Pamela J. Hastings

Sterling Publishing Co., Inc.
New York

A Sterling/Sewing Information Resources Book

Sewing Information Resources

Owner: JoAnn Pugh-Gannon
Photography: Kaz Ayukawa, K Graphics, and Geoffrey Gross, Geoffrey Gross
Photography, and Michael Mundy
Book Design and Electronic Page Layout: Ernie Shelton, Shelton Design Studios
Watercolor Illustrations: Jean Knudsen, JMKDesigns
Index: Mary Helen Schiltz

Library of Congress Cataloging-in-Publication Data

A Sterling/Sewing Information Resources Book

2 4 6 8 10 9 7 5 3 1

First paperback edition published in 2002 by
Sterling Publishing Company, Inc.
387 Park Avenue South, New York, N.Y. 10016
Produced by Sewing Information Resources
P.O. Box 330, Wasco, IL 60183
© 2001 by Pamela J. Hastings
Distributed in Canada by Sterling Publishing
C/o Canadian Manda Group, One Atlantic Avenue, Suite 105
Toronto, Ontario, Canada M6K 3E7
Distributed in Australia by Capricorn Link (Australia) Pty. Ltd.
P.O. Box 704, Windsor, NSW 2756 Australia
Printed in China
All rights reserved

Sterling ISBN 0-8069-0193-4 Hardcover
        ISBN 1-4027-0076-8 Paperback

FOR CLAUDIA ANNE

Acknowledgements

Special thanks to all my "behind the scenes" friends who helped create this book. To Kathy Sauter—for her beautiful sewing and extra-special details on the projects (They add a few extra steps, but are worth the extra time!). To Jean Knudsen—for sewing projects with my vague directions and for her incredible watercolor illustrations. I just love them! To Nancy Jewell—for providing sewing equipment from Viking Sewing Machine Company and for her usual encouragement. To Geoffrey Gross—for shooting great shots in an unusually chaotic setting. To Kaz Ayukawa and Ernie Shelton—for their usual great photos and page layouts. To

JoAnn Pugh-Gannon—for once again helping me get my projects from a file of ideas to an actual book. To my not-so-behind-the-scenes, not-so-helpful helpers, Christopher and Connor—for being as well-behaved as two little boys possibly could be on a three-day photo shoot at our house. And to my husband Geof—for being very patient as he climbed over props, fabric samples, and who knows what else, as this book was created by a pregnant woman with drastic mood swings!

TABLE OF CONTENTS

INTRODUCTION

When you think of covering a piece of furniture, the first thing that comes to mind is a traditional fitted slipcover for a worn chair or sofa. But if you take a quick tour of your home, you will discover endless possibilities for creating new looks with simple cover-ups.

Why a cover-up or slipcover?

Why not! A cover-up is simply a furniture face-lift. It can provide a quick fix plus add a few extra years to a worn-out dining table or create a new use for an inexpensive shelving unit.

What should I cover?

Virtually anything in your home can be changed and covered with a bit of fabric, a sewing machine, and some imagination. Tables and chairs can be given endless new looks changing with the seasons, the holidays, or special occasions. Tablecloths can be full, fitted, short, or long. They can be used as a slipcover to cover a dining table that is worn or dated (exactly as I did in my own dining room). Or what could be more fun than creating a special birthday tablecloth for someone special.

Chairs can also benefit from a bit of new fabric. Need some extra seating for a party? Why not cover an outdoor chair with a fabric that coordinates with your decor. Now that "odd" chair looks perfectly at home in its new surroundings. And what could be more inviting than a simple awning-stripe seat skirt to perk up your dated porch furniture.

Bedroom makeovers are quick and easy when you stitch up a coordinating duvet cover and pillow sham. A duvet cover is simply a large (You guessed it!) cover-up that can change an existing comforter from boring to beautiful. And, make the duvet cover reversible for seasonal changes. Add shams over your bed pillows and cover your old accent pillows with something new for the perfectly designed room.

Are you in need of extra storage areas? Simply cover up items you might not traditionally think of covering to easily create secret storage areas in unexpected spots. A simple roman shade attached to the front of a bookshelf looks great in the corner of a family room or den, and keeps the extra clutter of children's toys hidden from view. A sofa table can double as a buffet or server in the dining room with a floor length cover-up. It also provides extra storage for china or serving pieces. Disguise an ugly metal filing cabinet with a cover to match your room's decor. Covering furniture or storage pieces in your home not only adds new life to existing items, but is a great way to decorate on a budget.

So read on and enjoy. The projects in this book are suited to every sewing level from beginner to expert. Happy re-decorating!

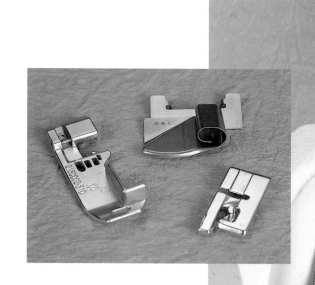

CHAPTER 1

THE BASICS

Before you begin any home decorating project you should familiarize yourself with some basic sewing techniques, presser feet, supplies, and notions. Using the proper technique and equipment will not only make your sewing easier and more pleasurable, but you are sure to be satisfied with your results. Some of the more common and essential techniques and equipment are listed here.

SEWING TECHNIQUES

HEMS

SERGER ROLLED HEM

A serger or overlock machine creates a narrow rolled hem on the edge of a single layer of fabric. It is ideal for finishing the edges of table toppers and chair seat skirts.

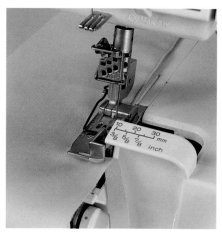

Set your serger for a rolled hem following your instruction manual. Cut the fabric ½" longer than the desired finished length. Run the single layer of fabric through the serger, trimming off the excess ½".

COVERSTITCH HEM

Some sergers may be set to sew a coverstitch. This hem has two or three rows of topstitching on the right side of the fabric and a flat overlock stitch covering the raw edge of your hem on the reverse side.

Set the serger for a coverstitch as directed in your instruction manual. Cut the fabric 1" to 2" longer than the finished length. Turn the hem up to the wrong side and press. Stitch the hem with the right side of your fabric facing up. Begin stitching a distance equal to the depth of the hem from the edge.

SERGER BLIND HEM

A blind hem is a great option for projects where you prefer not to have hem stitching show on the right side of your fabric. A blind hem may be sewn with a serger or a conventional sewing machine.

When using a serger blind hem, add the depth of the hem when calculating the length of your project.

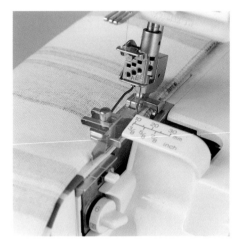

Set the serger for a blind hem as directed in your instruction manual. Fold the hem up to the wrong side of the fabric and press.

Fold the hem back on itself to the right side. The raw edge of the fabric should be even with the folded edge. Run the hem through the serger, with the needle just piercing the raw and folded edges of the fabric.

DOUBLE-FOLD BLIND HEM

When using a double-fold blind hem, add twice the depth of the hem when calculating the length of your project. For example, a chair skirt with a finished 1" double-fold hem requires a 2" hem allowance.

Set the sewing machine for a blind hem stitch and attach a blind hem foot. Fold the hem up the desired amount and press. Fold the hem up again the same amount; press.

Fold the double-fold hem back on itself to the right side of the fabric. With the wrong side of the fabric facing up, stitch the blind hem so the swing of the needle just pierces the fold of the fabric.

continued

STRAIGHT-STITCHED DOUBLE-FOLD HEM

A double-fold hem may also be stitched in place with a straight stitch.

Prepare the hem in the same manner as the Double-Fold Blind Hem, page 13. Straight-stitch the hem in place from the wrong side close to the fold.

NARROW HEM

This hem is similar to a double-fold hem, however it is much narrower. You will use a narrow hemming foot or hemming attachment on your sewing machine to create this hem.

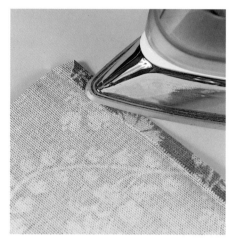

Attach a narrow hemmer to the sewing machine. Fold the hem up twice and press.

Place the folded edge of the fabric under the presser foot and sew a few stitches. Leaving the needle in the fabric, lift the presser foot and guide the fold of the fabric into the scroll of the foot. Lower the foot and continue sewing, holding the fabric straight and slightly taut in front of the foot.

PIPING

Custom piping is easy to make and adds a decorative accent on the edges of pillows, chair skirts, and fitted cover-ups.

PLAIN PIPING

Plain piping is a smooth fabric-wrapped cord inserted between layers of fabric.

Fold a bias strip of fabric, right side out, around a cord. With the raw edges even, machine-baste close to the cord using a zipper foot. To determine the width of the bias strip, measure the circumference of the cord and add 1" for seam allowances.

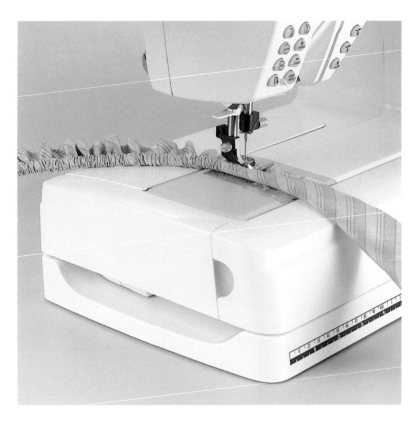

SHIRRED PIPING

Shirred piping is a bias strip of fabric gathered around the length of the cord.

Fold a bias strip around a cord and stitch horizontally across one end of the cord to secure. Using a zipper foot, stitch close to the cord for 3" or 4". Leaving the needle in the fabric, lift the presser foot and pull on the cord to shirr the fabric. Lower the presser foot and sew another 3" to 4". Repeat this procedure until the entire cord is covered.

ATTACHING GROMMETS

Use grommets as a decorative accent when a project requires ties or tassels.

Fold the edge of the fabric to the wrong side and press. Mark the placement of the grommets and cut the opening using the grommet tool. Insert the "male" side of the grommet through the fabric from the right to the wrong side.

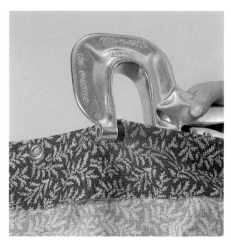

Place the securing ring over the grommet post and press together.

PRESSER FEET

A wide variety of presser feet are available for most sewing machines. Using specialty feet designed for specific sewing techniques is very helpful when creating home decorating projects.

The *gathering foot* (C) gathers a single layer of fabric. It can also be used to gather one layer of fabric to a flat piece of fabric.

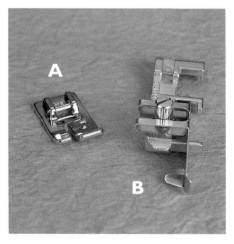

A *blind hem* foot is available for both the sewing machine (A) and the serger (B). These feet allow for accurate fabric placement so that stitching is not readily seen on the right side of the fabric. Use these feet for the blind hem techniques previously described in this chapter.

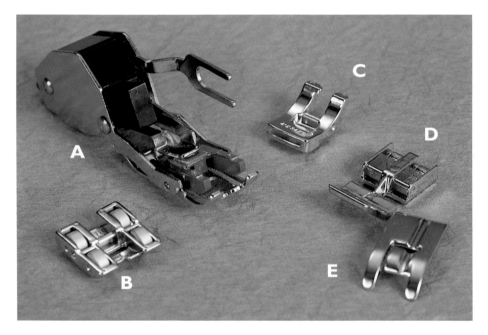

The *even-feed foot* (A) has rubber teeth similar to the feed dogs on the machine. These rubber teeth work in tandem with the feed dogs to ensure that both layers of fabric feed evenly through the sewing machine. This foot is particularly helpful when sewing long lengths of fabric together.

A *roller foot* (B), as the name implies, has rollers on the underside. This foot is perfect for sewing over laminated fabric.

A *zipper foot* (D) is designed to be used on either side of the needle and allows for positioning the needle close to the cording or zipper teeth.

A *piping foot* (E) has a groove on the underside of the foot that easily rides over narrow piping as you are sewing. The needle enters the fabric close to the cord.

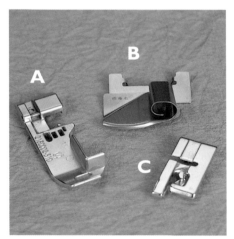

The *rolled hem* foot is designed so that the fabric edge is turned under and stitched simultaneously. It is available for the serger (A) and comes in various widths for sewing machines (B & C).

SUPPLIES & NOTIONS

As with the presser feet, the right sewing supplies and notions will make your decorating projects more pleasurable to sew. A wide variety of decorative trims are also available to give your projects a one-of-a-kind distinctive look.

A *bias tape maker* is a tool you will find invaluable for making coordinating or contrasting bias binding. Cut bias strips of fabric the desired width, slide these strips through the bias tape maker, and the edges are automatically folded in the correct amount. Press the edges in place and the bias strips are ready for stitching. This tool is available in a number of sizes.

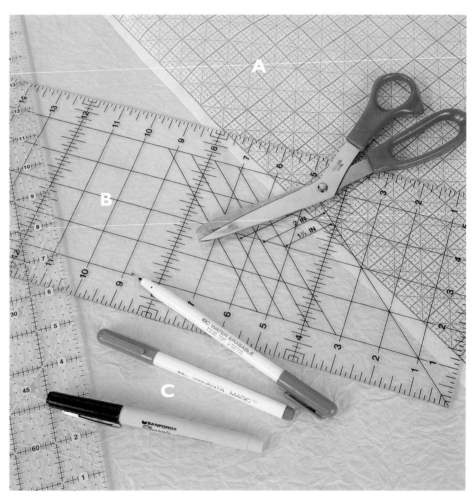

Pattern or tracing paper (A) is essential when designing cover-ups. Use it for tracing tabletops, chair seats, or other pieces of furniture to be covered. The grid pattern makes adding seam allowances very easy.

Clear plastic grided rulers (B), traditionally used for quilting, are perfect for adding accurate hems and seam allowances, and making patterns.

Marking pens (C) have a variety of uses in home decorating projects. Use permanent markers for pattern-making and water- or air-soluble markers for marking hems, stitching lines, or other important guidelines. These marks can easily be removed, though test your markings on a scrap of fabric first.

continued

17

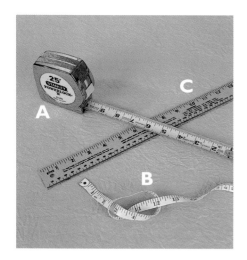

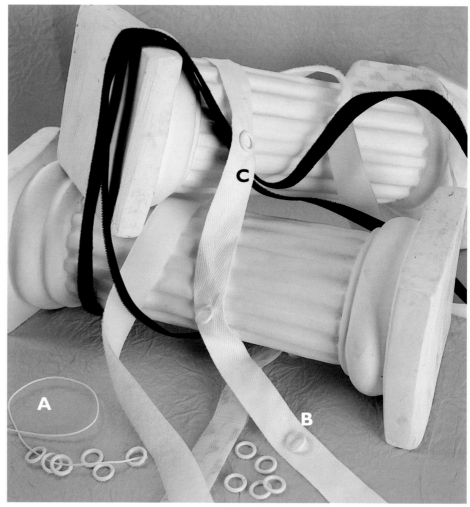

Metal tape measures (A) are useful when measuring large areas such as tabletops and are needed to accurately measure the height of tables, bookshelves, or other tall objects.

Because of their flexibility, *cloth tape measures* (B) are great for measuring the circumference of stools and for measuring soft items like pillows.

A *yardstick* (C), either metal or wood, is 36" long and is handy for measuring smaller items as well as fabric.

Some notions are not visible on completed projects, but are essential in construction. *Rings or ring tape* (A & B) are sewn to the reverse side of roman shades. A cord is then run through the rings to raise and lower the shade.

Hook and loop tape (C) comes in a variety of weights, types, and colors to suit your decorating projects. Use a lightweight sew-

on tape for closures on duvet covers or pillow shams. Velcro® brand Half & Half™ tape is perfect for attaching fabric to a hard surface, such as a skirt to a vanity table. One side of the tape is sewn to the wrong side of the fabric, the other side of the tape has an adhesive backing and will adhere to a hard surface.

Cording with lip (A) is twisted cording attached to a woven or gimp edging. The edging is enclosed in the seam while sewing and the cording shows on the right side of the fabric where the seams meet. This cording is available in a wide range of colors and textures.

Uncovered cord (B) is available in a variety of diameters and is used when making custom plain or shirred piping.

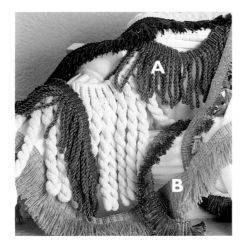

Bullion fringe (A) is made up of softly twisted yarns hanging down from the woven or braided edging. Bullion fringe is available in a

variety of textures and widths and is anywhere from 3" to 9" in length. Use bullion fringe to trim the edges of tablecloths and chair skirts, or for a unique edging on pillows.

Brush fringe (B) is a type of fringe with loose threads hanging off a braided or woven edge. This fringe is also made from a variety of fibers and textures.

Tassels (A) may be used to accent the corners of pillows or attach them to a button for a decorative accent.

Chair ties (B) are small tassels joined by a length of cord and may be used in place of fabric ties at the back of seat skirts or to join two sides of a cover-up.

Ric rac (A) is a great trim for a more casual look. It may be sewn directly onto a table topper or into the edge of a seam in the same manner as piping for an interesting edging.

Ribbons (B) come in an endless variety of fabrics, colors, and patterns. There are ribbons available to suit every and any project. Use grosgrain or plaid ribbons to add interest to the hem of a project or to highlight decorative embroideries. A sheer ribbon provides an elegant look when used as the tie along the edges of pillows or bench covers.

Grommets (C) provide a unique alternative to buttonholes or ties enclosed in a seam. Attach grommets along the edge and thread ribbon or cording through the holes for a creative way to close an opening.

CHAPTER 2

TABLE FOR TWO

Tablecloths are one of the easiest home decorating projects to sew and can add just the right touch to any setting. Round tablecloths are perfect for covering up a worn picnic table for an elegant summer party. Use round accent tables with coordinating toppers to add an inexpensive end table to a room.

What better way to rejuvenate old dining room furniture than by creating a floor length cloth to slipcover your existing table, giving it an updated look? Functional and practical tablecloths are the perfect cover-ups for adding just the right touch to finish any room.

MEASURING TABLES & CALCULATING YARDAGE

To determine the measurement of a tablecloth, the dimensions of the tabletop are added to a drop length. The drop length is the measurement from the edge of the table to the desired finished length of the tablecloth. The most popular drop lengths are:

Floor length—measure from the edge of the table to within $1/2$" of the floor

Dining length—measure from the edge of the table to 1" of the chair seat

Formal length—measure from the edge of the table to a drop of 18" to 24"

Calculating Yardage for a Round Tablecloth

FINISHED DIAMETER OF THE TABLECLOTH

A. Diameter of table _____ +

B. Add 2 X the drop length _____ =

C. Finished diameter: _____

CALCULATE YARDAGE

D. Finished diameter (C) + hems _____ ÷

E. Divided by fabric width _____ =

F. Number of widths _____

G. Multiply number of widths by diameter (C) _____

H. Yardage required: (G) divided by 36" _____

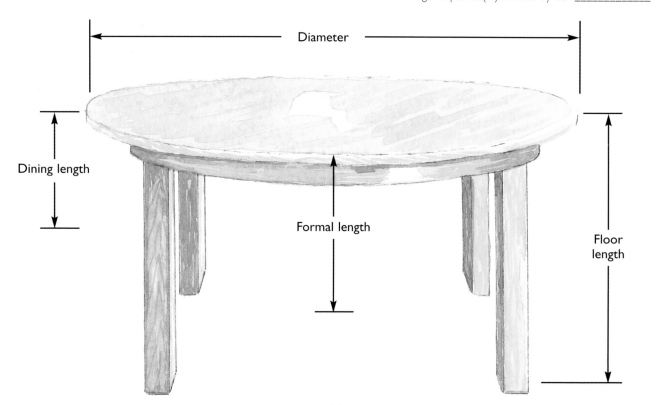

Diameter

Dining length

Formal length

Floor length

Calculating Yardage for a Rectangular Tablecloth

CUT LENGTH OF THE TABLECLOTH

A. Measure the length of the table _____ +

B. Add twice the drop length plus hem _____ =

C. Cut length of tablecloth _____

CUT WIDTH OF THE TABLECLOTH

D. Measure the width of the table _____ +

E. Add twice the drop length plus hem _____ =

F. Cut width of tablecloth _____

G. Cut width (F) divided by fabric width = _____

CALCULATE YARDAGE

H. Cut length of tablecloth (C) _____ x

I. Multiply by number of widths (G) _____ =

J. Total length: _____

K. Yardage required: (J) divided by 36" _____

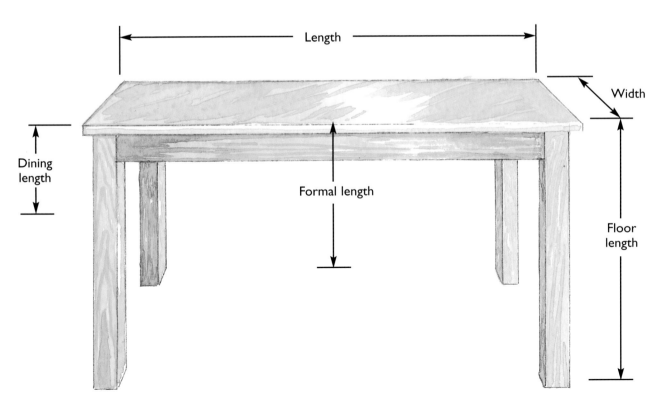

ROUND TABLECLOTH
GARDEN DELIGHT

YOU WILL NEED:

- Decorator fabric
- Measuring tape
- String
- T-pin
- Fabric marker

1 Measure the diameter of the table and the desired drop length (see Measuring Tables & Calculating Yardage, page 22). Cut the fabric, according to your calculations. If the tablecloth diameter is wider than the fabric, piecing will be necessary (see Matching Prints, Chapter 4).

2 Stitch the fabric panels together to form a large square. Use one fabric width in the center and then divide the additional required width in half, sewing a panel of equal width to either side of the center panel.

24

3 Fold the fabric in half lengthwise and then crosswise into quarters, matching the raw edges. Pin through all the layers to hold the fabric in place.

4 Cut a string to half the diameter of the table. Tie one end of the string to a marking pen and secure the opposite end of the string to the folded corner of the fabric with a T-pin. Draw along the fabric, creating a curved line for cutting.

5 Cut along the marked line and hem the tablecloth with a narrow hem or a serger rolled hem.

continued

1 Measure the table top and the desired drop length (see Measuring Tables & Calculating Yardage, page 22). Cut the fabric based on your calculations. If the width of the tablecloth is wider than the fabric width, it will be necessary to piece the fabric to reach the required width (see Matching Prints, Chapter 4).

2 Stitch the fabric panels together using one full fabric width for the center of the tablecloth. Divide any additional required width in half and stitch panels of equal measurement to the long edges of the center panel, matching any pattern if necessary.

3 Fold the tablecloth in half lengthwise, then crosswise. Place a round plate in the one corner with the four raw edges. Trace along the plate edge with a fabric marker. Cut along the marked line.

4 Turn up a ½" double-fold hem along the edge (see Hems, Chapter 1) and topstitch in place.

RECTANGULAR TABLECLOTH
A SIMPLE BREAKFAST

YOU WILL NEED:

- Decorator fabric
- Round plate
- Fabric marker

1   Measure the table and cut the fabric according to the instructions (see Measuring Tables & Calculating Yardage, page 22).

2   Cut a bias strip of the contrasting fabric, using the circumference of the tablecloth by 2" wide for the bias strips. Pull the bias strip through the bias strip maker with the wrong side up and press the raw edges in place.

TABLECLOTH WITH BIAS BINDING
PORCH APPEAL

YOU WILL NEED:

- Decorator fabric for tablecloth
- Contrasting fabric for bias binding
- Bias tape maker

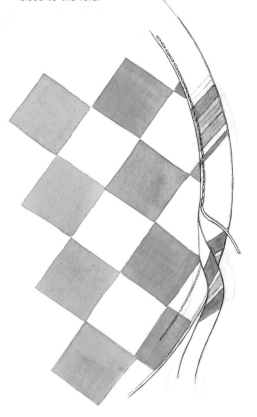

4 Fold the band to the right side of the tablecloth, press and pin in place. Topstitch close to the fold.

3 Open out one raw edge of the bias band. Pin the right side of the band to the wrong side of the tablecloth. Stitch in place along the crease line. Trim the seam.

29

SQUARE TOPPER WITH TRIM
TOP IT OFF

YOU WILL NEED:

- Decorator fabric
- Ric rac trim equal to eight times the length of one side of the table topper.
- Basting tape or glue stick
- Ruler or yardstick
- Fabric marker

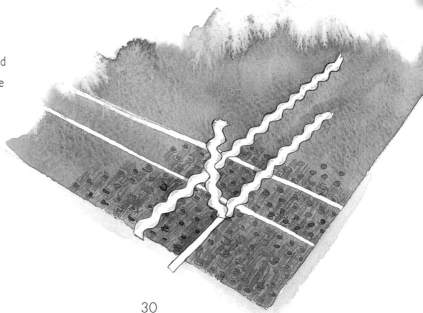

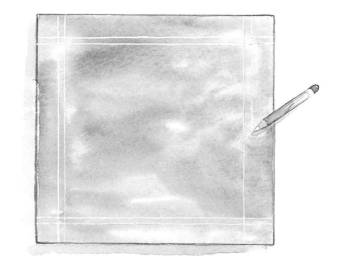

1 Cut the table topper to the desired size square plus 2" for hems. Using a fabric marker, mark the placement for the ric rac trim 2¹/₂" in from the edge. Mark a second line 3¹/₂" in from the cut edge.

2 Place the ric rac trim over the marked lines and secure in place with basting tape or a glue stick.

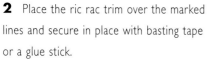

30

3 With your sewing machine set to a short straight stitch, stitch down the center of the ric rac trim.

4 Turn up a ¹/₂" double-fold hem (see Double-Fold Hem, Chapter 1) on all edges and topstitch in place.

1 Cut the topper to the desired length plus 2" by the desired width plus 2".

2 Turn up a $\frac{1}{2}$" double-fold hem on all sides of the table topper (see Double-Fold Hem, Chapter 1) and press.

EMBROIDERED TOPPER
EMBROIDERY MAGIC

YOU WILL NEED:

- Decorator fabric
- Ribbon equal to the measurement of each side of the cloth plus 12"
- Rayon embroidery thread
- Embroidery design
- Tear-away stabilizer
- Fabric marker

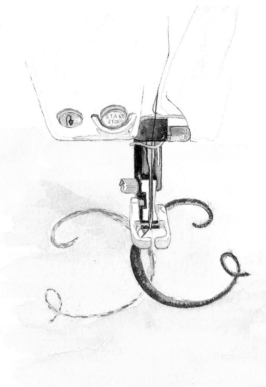

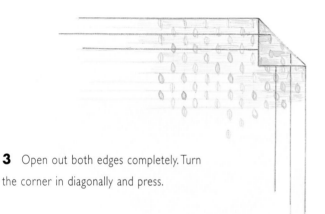

3 Open out both edges completely. Turn the corner in diagonally and press.

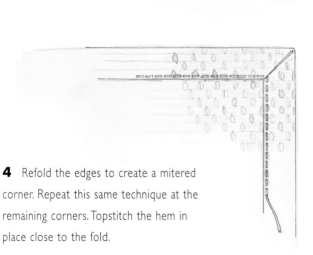

4 Refold the edges to create a mitered corner. Repeat this same technique at the remaining corners. Topstitch the hem in place close to the fold.

5 Embroider a monogram or motif in the desired location on the table topper (see Embellishments, Chapter 6).

6 Mark the location for the ribbon placement and stitch in place (see Embellishments, Chapter 6).

33

TABLECLOTH WITH MITERED BAND
ELEGANTLY BANDED

YOU WILL NEED:

- Decorator fabric
- Contrasting fabric for mitered band

1 Cut the tablecloth to the desired size plus 1". Cut two contrasting bands to the desired width plus 1" by the length of the tablecloth. Cut the remaining two bands to the desired width plus 1" by the width of the tablecloth.

2 Press under ½" to the wrong side of one long edge of each contrasting band.

3 With the right sides of the bands to the wrong side of the fabric, pin two bands to the opposite sides of the tablecloth. Stitch with a ½" seam allowance.

continued

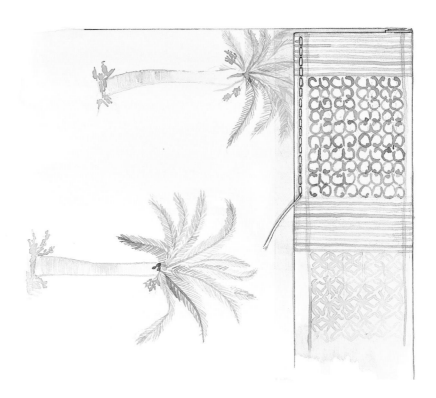

4 Turn the bands to the right side of the tablecloth and press. Stitch close to the fold.

5 Pin the remaining bands to the tablecloth, the right side of the bands to the wrong side of the cloth. Begin and end stitching $1/2$" from the short sides of the bands.

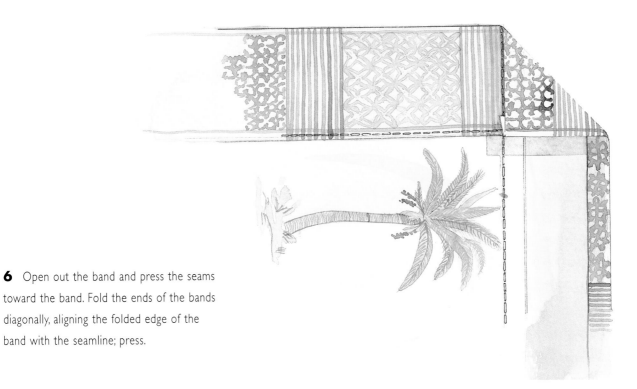

6 Open out the band and press the seams toward the band. Fold the ends of the bands diagonally, aligning the folded edge of the band with the seamline; press.

7 Fold the band to the right side of the tablecloth and topstitch the band in place, close to the mitered and folded edges.

FITTED TABLECLOTH WITH CONTRASTING BAND
A ROMANTIC EVENING

YOU WILL NEED:

- Decorator fabric
- Contrasting fabric for lower edge of skirt
- Pattern tracing paper

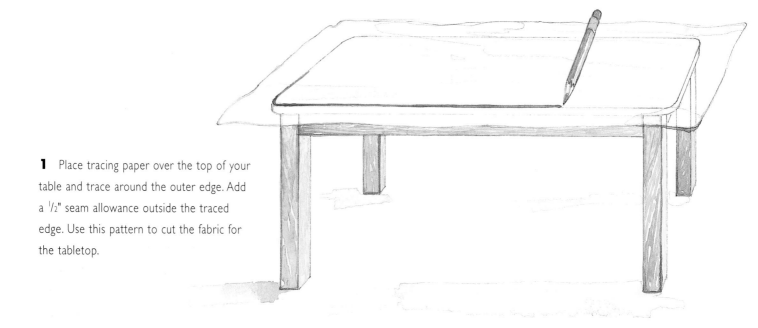

1 Place tracing paper over the top of your table and trace around the outer edge. Add a ½" seam allowance outside the traced edge. Use this pattern to cut the fabric for the tabletop.

2 To determine the measurement of the skirt, measure each side of the table and add together. Add 24" to this measurement for the corner pleats. Cut the skirt fabric to this measurement by the drop length of the tablecloth minus 2½". Piece the fabric together along the short edges to form one continuous skirt piece. Press the seam allowances open.

3 Cut the contrasting band according to the outer measurement of the table plus 24" (as for the skirt) by 7" wide. Sew the band together along the short edges to form one continuous loop. Fold the band in half with the wrong sides together and press with the raw edges even.

continued

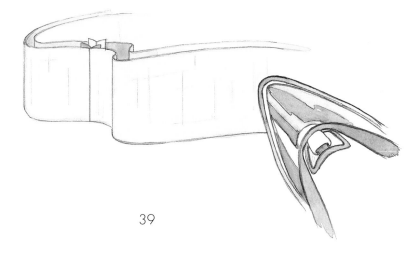

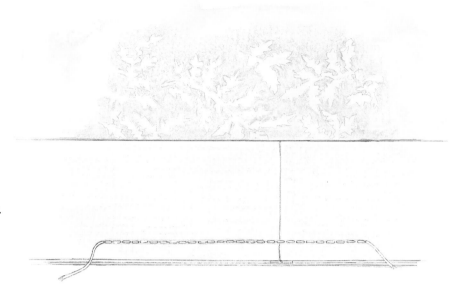

4 Sew the band to the bottom edge of the skirt with right sides together. Clean-finish the seam with a serger or zigzag stitch. Press the seam allowance toward the skirt.

5 Make a 6" box pleat in one corner of the tablecloth (see Chair Skirt with Pleated Corners, Chapter 3). Press the pleat in place.

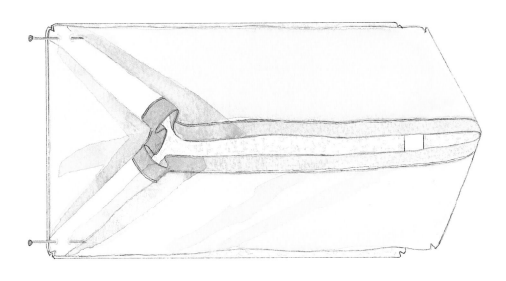

6 To determine the placement of the next pleat, measure along the top edge of the skirt from the center of the completed pleat to a point equal to the measurement of the short side of the table plus 6". Make the two remaining pleats by measuring from the center of the completed pleats, along the top edge of the skirt to a point equal to the measurement of the remaining long and short edges of the table plus 6". Mark these points as the center of the pleats.

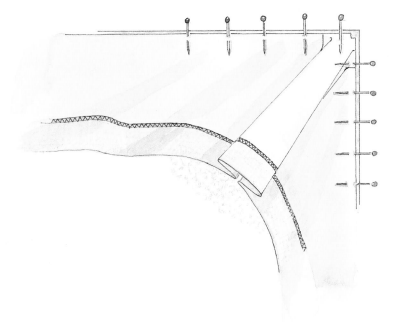

7 Pin the pleated table skirt to the top piece, matching the center of each pleat to each corner of the top. Stitch in place with a $1/2$" seam allowance.

CHAPTER 3

HAVE A SEAT

How often have you added a desk chair or folding chair around your Thanksgiving table, only to find that your perfectly set table no longer looked perfect with that mismatched chair? The solution—try slipcovers or easy cover-ups that will turn any mismatched chair into a perfectly coordinated addition to your room. Slipcovers may cover an entire chair or just the seat or back. Floor length or short, formal or casual, slipcovers and cover-ups can turn an ordinary chair or stool into the perfect seat for any occasion.

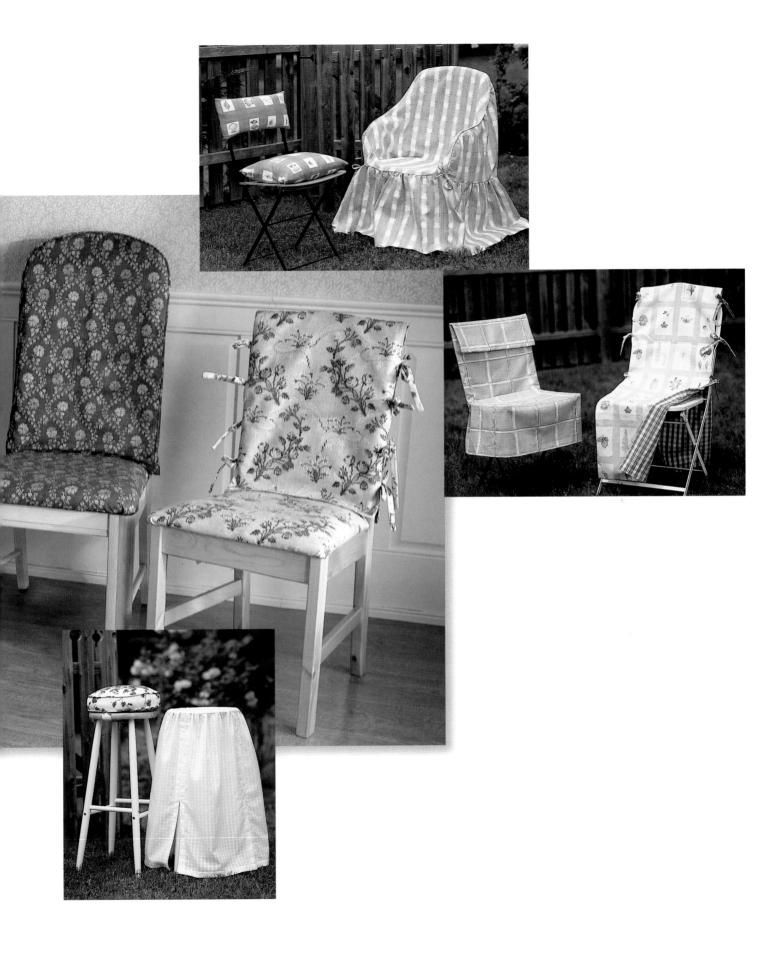

MAKING A PATTERN

Chair cover-ups can be made in a wide variety of styles. Some require just a few measurements, while others will need a pattern to ensure a proper fit.

Seat Patterns

1 Place tracing paper on the chair seat and trace around the outermost edge of the seat. Be sure to mark the location where the back spindles meet the seat.

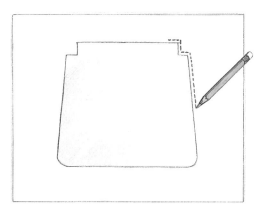

2 Add a $1/2$" seam allowance around the outside edge of the pattern tracing.

Chair Back Pattern

1 Lay your tracing paper on a flat surface. Place the chair on the tracing paper with the back of the chair lying on the paper. Trace around the chair back. Mark a line on the pattern where the chair back meets the seat.

2 Add a $1/2$"-1" seam allowance around the outside edge of the pattern tracing depending on the thickness of the chair back. Add twice the desired hem depth to the bottom edge of the pattern piece.

1 Make a pattern for the chair seat (see Making a Pattern, page 44) and cut out two seat pieces. (Note: One piece will be used for lining.)

CHAIR SKIRT WITH PLEATED CORNERS
SIMPLE PLEATS

YOU WILL NEED:

- Decorator fabric
- Pattern tracing paper
- Marking pen
- Fabric marker

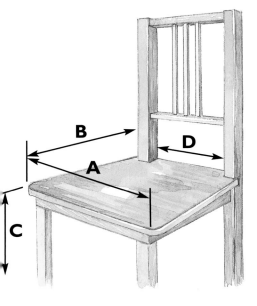

2 Cut the fabric for the skirt front and sides to the measurement of the front (A) and sides of the seat (B) plus 24" by the desired length (C) plus 1". For the skirt back, measure across the back of the seat (D), between the spindles adding 1" by the desired length plus 1". Cut the skirt lining to same measurements.

3 Sew the skirt to the skirt lining, right sides together, along the bottom and sides of skirt. Trim the seams, turn right side out and press. Machine-baste along the top edge of the skirt. Repeat with the skirt back.

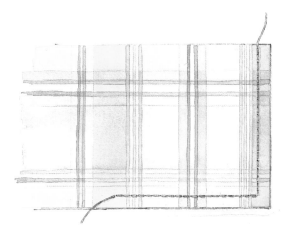

4 To determine the location for the corner pleats, fold the skirt fabric in half crosswise and mark at the fold. (Note: This is the center point of the front of the skirt.) From this marked point, measure out to each side one-half the measurement of the seat front plus 6" and make a clip mark.

continued

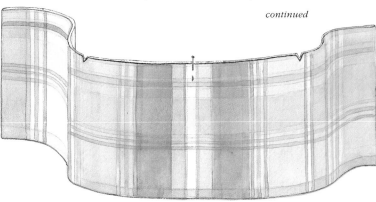

5 Measure out 6" to each side of the clip marks and mark with a fabric marker or pin.

6 Bring the markings together at the clip mark, folding the pleats in place. Press the pleats and machine-baste across the top edge to hold.

7 To make the ties, cut four pieces 2" × 8". Fold each tie piece in half lengthwise and press. Open out each piece and fold the long edges in to meet to the center crease. Press again. Fold in half and topstitch close to the edge of each tie, tucking in ½" at one end.

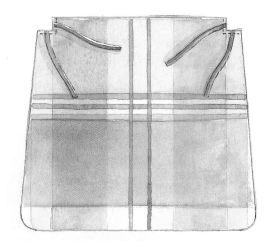

8 Pin the ties in place in each back corner ³/₄" from the edges on the right side of the seat piece. Machine-baste in place.

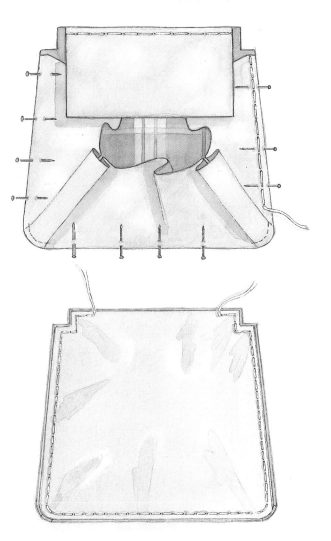

9 Pin the skirt pieces to the seat, right sides together, placing the ends of the skirt ¹/₂" in from the back edges of the seat. Match the center of the pleats with the corner of the seat. Machine-baste in place.

10 Layer the seat lining over the pinned skirt pieces, right sides together. Stitch the seat lining and seat, right sides together, leaving an opening for turning. Turn right side out and slipstitch the opening closed.

RUFFLED SEAT SKIRT
PATIO PERFECT

YOU WILL NEED:

- Decorator fabric
- Lining fabric
- Contrasting fabric for piping and ties
- Cording
- Pattern tracing paper
- Marking pen
- Fabric marker

1 Make a pattern for the seat (see Making a Pattern, page 44). Cut one seat piece from the fabric and one from the lining.

2 Measure around the sides and front of the seat. Cut the skirt fabric two and one-half times this measurement by the desired skirt length plus 1$\frac{1}{2}$". Piece the fabric as needed.

3 Cut a second skirt piece two and one-half times the measurement of the back of the seat between the spindles by the desired length plus 1$\frac{1}{2}$".

4 Make covered piping (see Plain Piping, Chapter 1) from the contrasting fabric equal to the outer measurement of the seat plus 2". Baste the piping to the edges of the skirt (see Chair Back Slipcover, page 54).

5 From the contrasting fabric, cut four ties 2" × 12". Make the ties and baste in place (see Chair Skirt with Pleated Corners, page 46).

6 Make a $\frac{1}{2}$" double-fold hem along the bottom and sides of the skirt pieces.

7 Stitch two rows of machine basting along the top edge of the skirt. Gather the top edge of the skirt.

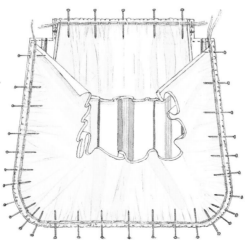

8 Pin the skirt to the seat, right sides together, and adjust the gathers. Place the ends of the skirt $^{1}/_{2}$" in from the back edges. Stitch with a $^{1}/_{2}$" seam allowance and press the seam toward the seat.

9 Complete the seat cover as directed in Chair Skirt with Pleated Corners, page 46 (see steps 5 and 6).

1 Make a pattern for the seat (see Making a Pattern, page 44) and cut out one seat from the fabric and one from the lining.

2 Measure around the front and sides of the seat and cut the skirt to this measurement by the desired length plus 1". (Note: Cut the fabric ½" to 1" below the motif you will be using as the shape at the bottom of the hem.)

3 Pin the skirt and lining, right sides together, and baste along the side and bottom edges.

4 With the wrong side of the fabric facing up, select a "design line" to use as a stitching guide. (Note: We chose the bananas as our bottom shape.) Stitch along the edge of the selected motif and stitch a ½" seam allowance along the side edges.

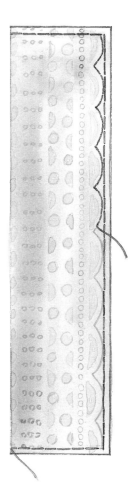

Seat Cover with Shaped Hem
FRESH FRUIT

YOU WILL NEED:

- Decorator fabric with a distinct pattern
- Lining fabric
- Marking pen
- Fabric marker
- Pattern tracing paper

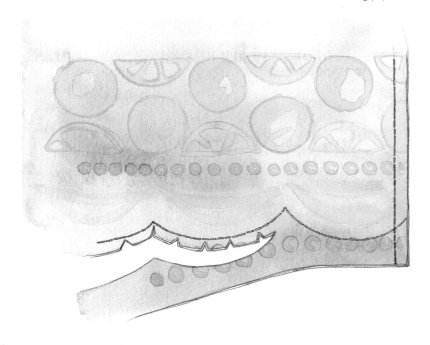

7 Make ties and complete the skirt (see Chair Skirt with Pleated Corners, page 46, eliminating the steps for the pleats).

5 Trim the seams and clip the curves.

6 Turn the skirt right side out and press. Baste along the top edge of the skirt.

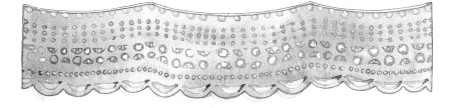

CHAIR BACK SLIPCOVER
DINING PLEASURE

YOU WILL NEED:

• Decorator fabric

• Pattern tracing paper

• Cording or decorative trim equal to the
outside measurement of the chair back plus 2"

• Marking pen

• Fabric marker

1 Trace the chair back (see Making a Pattern, page 44) adding a 1" seam allowance to the sides and top of the chair back and 2" at the bottom of the pattern for hems. Cut two back pieces from the fabric.

2 If using custom piping, make piping as directed in Chapter 1.

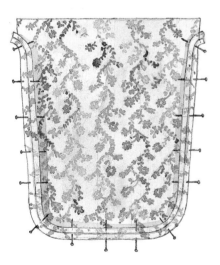

3 Pin the piping to the outer edge of the chair back keeping the raw edge of the piping even with the raw edge of the fabric.

4 Using a zipper foot, baste the piping in place close to the cord.

54

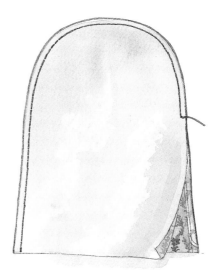

5 Place the front and back, right sides together, and stitch with a $1/2$" seam allowance.

6 Turn up and press a 1" double-fold hem along the bottom edge of the chair back. Stitch the hem in place.

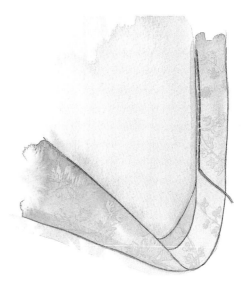

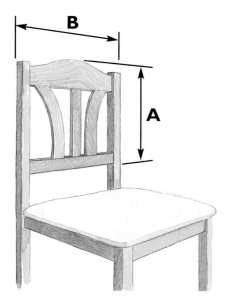

1 Measure the chair back (see Making a Pattern, page 44) and cut four fabric pieces the height of the chair back (A) plus 1" by the width of the chair back (B) plus 1". (Note: Two pieces will be used for the lining.) Cut 12 tie pieces 1½" x 10".

CHAIR BACK COVER-UP WITH TIES
TIE IT UP

YOU WILL NEED:

- Decorator fabric
- Marking pen
- Fabric marker

2 With right sides together, stitch two fabric pieces along the top edge with a $\frac{1}{2}$" seam allowance. Press the seam open. Stitch the lining pieces together along the top edge. Press the seam open.

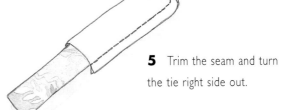

5 Trim the seam and turn the tie right side out.

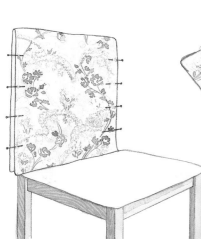

3 Place the cover over the chair back and mark the placement for the ties with pins or a fabric marker.

4 To make the ties, fold the fabric in half lengthwise and stitch with a $\frac{1}{2}$" seam allowance along the long edge and one short edge.

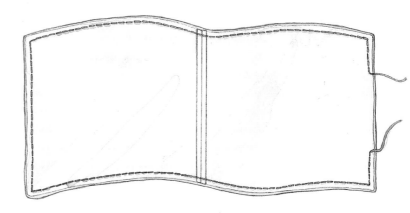

6 Baste the ties in place at the markings.

7 Stitch the lining and the chair back cover, right sides together, around all the edges with a $\frac{1}{2}$" seam allowance. Leave an opening for turning.

8 Trim the corners, turn the cover right side out, and slipstitch the opening closed.

Cover-up with Side Buttons
ELEGANT STRIPES

YOU WILL NEED:

- Decorator fabric
- Lining fabric
- Covered buttons
- Marking pen
- Fabric marker

1 Measure the chair back as you did for the Chair Back Cover-up with Ties, page 56. Cut two pieces of fabric the height of the chair back plus 2" by the width of the chair back plus 17". Cut two pieces of lining, the height of the chair back plus 2" by the width of the chair minus 9".

2 Sew the chair back pieces together along the top edge, right sides together, with a $^1/_2$ " seam allowance. Repeat with the lining pieces.

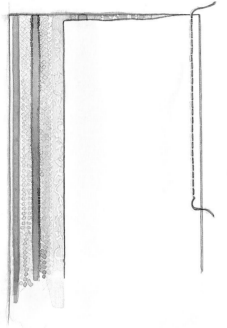

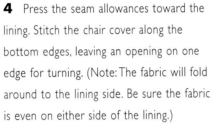

3 Sew the lining and fabric, right sides together, along the side seams using a $\frac{1}{2}$" seam allowance.

4 Press the seam allowances toward the lining. Stitch the chair cover along the bottom edges, leaving an opening on one edge for turning. (Note: The fabric will fold around to the lining side. Be sure the fabric is even on either side of the lining.)

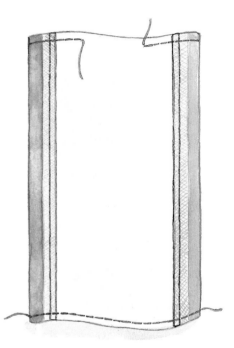

5 Trim the corners, turn the cover right side out, and slipstitch the opening closed. Press along each side edge of the chair back cover.

continued

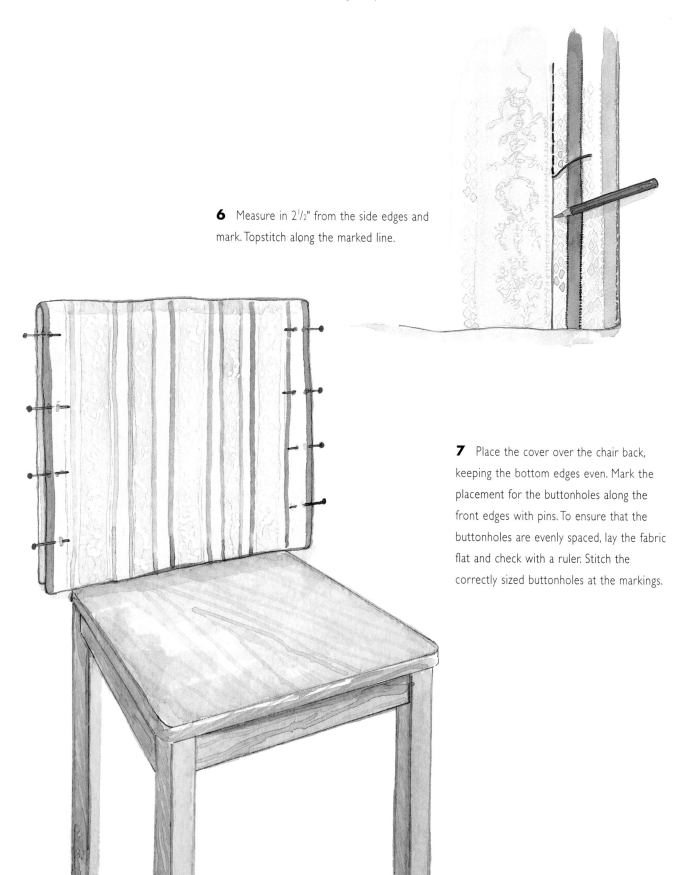

6 Measure in 2½" from the side edges and mark. Topstitch along the marked line.

7 Place the cover over the chair back, keeping the bottom edges even. Mark the placement for the buttonholes along the front edges with pins. To ensure that the buttonholes are evenly spaced, lay the fabric flat and check with a ruler. Stitch the correctly sized buttonholes at the markings.

8 Fold the chair back cover in half and mark the placement of the buttons along the inside back edges of the chair back cover.

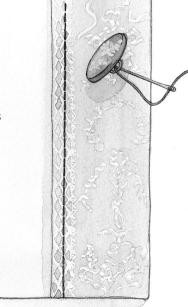

9 Cover the buttons according to the manufacturer's directions. Stitch the buttons in place along the inside edge of the chair back cover.

1 To make a rough pattern from muslin for the chair, cut muslin pieces as follows: for the back, cut 55" x 36"; for the front, cut 55" x 36"; and for the seat, cut 24" x 24".

2 Fold the muslin pieces in half crosswise and finger-press to mark the center. Draw a line along the fold and label the pieces— back, front, and seat.

SLIPCOVER FOR OUTDOOR CHAIR
PERFECT PICNICS

YOU WILL NEED:

• Decorator fabric
• 4 yards of muslin for seat pattern
• Fabric marker
• Marking pen
• Double-stick tape
• Cording

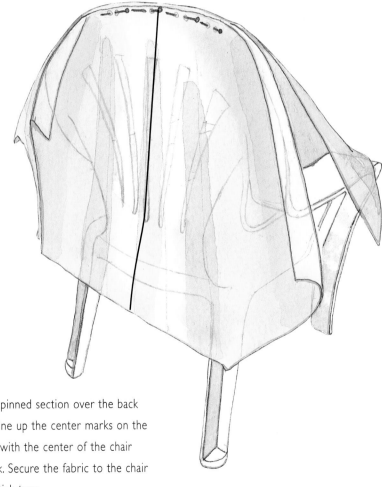

3 Pin the back and front muslin pieces together along the top center edge for a few inches.

4 Place the pinned section over the back of the chair. Line up the center marks on the muslin pieces with the center of the chair front and back. Secure the fabric to the chair with double-stick tape.

continued

63

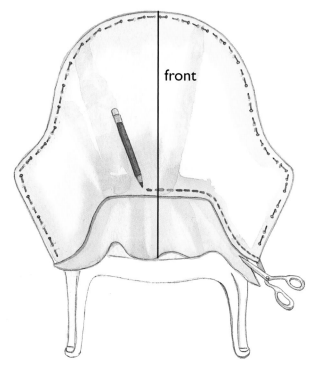

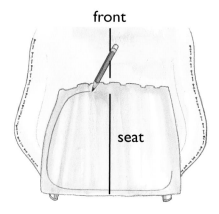

5 Drape the pattern piece around the back and arms of the chair, pinning to mark the seam allowance.

6 Mark the back edge of the seat along the bottom of the chair front piece. Trim away the excess muslin, about 1" from the marked line.

7 Place the seat section on the chair aligning the muslin on the seat where the chair back meets the seat. Secure the muslin in place with double-stick tape, lining up the marked line with the center of the seat. The fabric should fit comfortably across the seat, not pulled taut, to allow for sitting ease.

8 With the seat pattern piece in place, trace the outline of the seat and trim away the excess muslin about 1" from the seam.

9 Remove the muslin pattern from the chair and remove the pins. Cut the chair cover from your decorator fabric, using the center lines on the muslin as grainlines when cutting out your pattern.

10 For the skirt, cut the decorator fabric two-and-one-half times the measurement of the circumference of the seat by the desired skirt length plus 2$\frac{1}{2}$".

11 Make the piping as directed in Chapter 1. Baste the piping along the top and arm edge of the chair front.

12 Pin the chair front to the seat along the bottom edge of the chair front piece. Stitch with a $1/2$" seam allowance.

13 Pin the chair back to the chair front along the top and arm seams. Stitch in place with a $1/2$" seam allowance.

15 Turn up a 1" double-fold hem on the bottom edge of the skirt and stitch. Divide the skirt into quarters and mark with pins.

16 Pin the skirt to the body of the slipcover, right sides together, matching the markings. Pull up on the basting threads to gather. Stitch the skirt in place using a $1/2$" seam allowance.

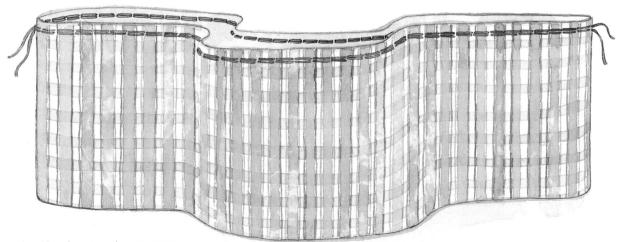

14 Sew the skirt piece together to create one continuous circle. Stitch two rows of basting stitches along the top edge within the $1/2$" seam allowance.

CAFÉ CHAIR COVER WITH FLAP
CAFÉ PLAID

YOU WILL NEED:

- Decorator fabric
- Marking pen
- Fabric marker

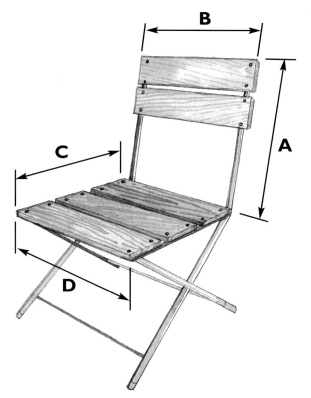

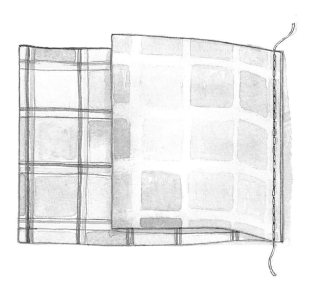

1 Measure the chair and cut the pattern pieces as follows: Cut two back pieces the height of the back (A) plus 7" by the width of the widest point of the back (B) plus 1". Cut one seat piece the depth of the seat (C) plus 1" by the width of the seat (D) plus 1". Cut one skirt piece the measurement of the seat front and sides (C + D) plus 1" by the desired skirt length plus 1¹/₂". Cut one back skirt piece the width of the seat (D) plus 1" by the desired skirt length plus 1¹/₂".

2 Stitch one chair back piece to the skirt back along the bottom edge, right sides together, using a ¹/₂" seam allowance.

3 Stitch the remaining chair back piece to the seat along the back edge of the seat, right sides together, and a ¹/₂" seam allowance.

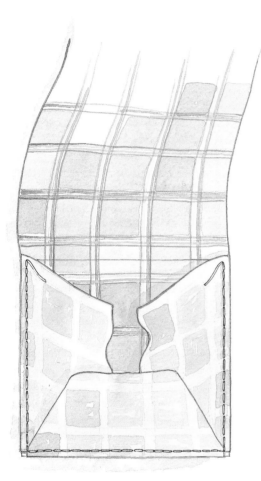

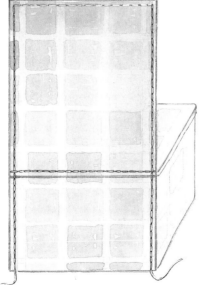

4 Pin the skirt to the seat along the sides and front, and stitch using a $1/2$" seam allowance.

5 Pin the chair back/skirt back piece to the chair front and the remaining back seams on the skirt. Stitch in place with a $1/2$" seam allowance.

6 Turn up and stitch a $1/2$" double-fold hem along the bottom edge of the skirt.

7 Slip the cover over the chair folding the excess fabric at the top of the chair back toward the front of the chair.

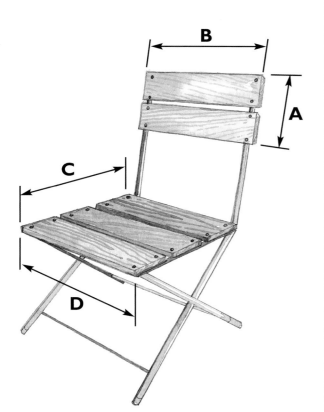

1 Cut two pieces of fabric the height (A) and width (B) of the bistro chair back plus 1". Cut two pieces of fabric the width (D) and depth (C) of the bistro chair seat plus 1". Cut strip of fabric the width of the chair back (B) plus 1½" by 8" and one strip of fabric the width of the seat (D) plus 1½" by 8".

Café Chair Cushions
BISTRO COMFORT

YOU WILL NEED:

• Decorator fabric

• Pillow forms—foam the size needed for cushions

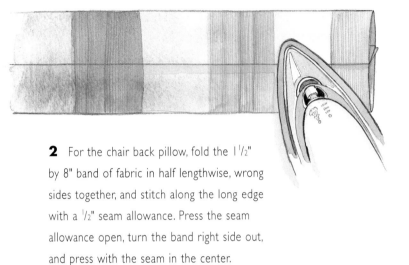

2 For the chair back pillow, fold the 1 1/2" by 8" band of fabric in half lengthwise, wrong sides together, and stitch along the long edge with a 1/2" seam allowance. Press the seam allowance open, turn the band right side out, and press with the seam in the center.

4 Stitch the chair back pieces, right sides together, with a 1/2" seam allowance leaving an opening for turning. Trim the corners and turn right side out. Insert the pillow form and slipstitch the opening closed.

5 Construct the seat pillow in the same manner; however, the band should be placed about 3"-4" from the front edge of the chair seat.

3 Center the band on the right side of one chair back piece. Baste along the edges of the band.

REVERSIBLE CAFÉ CHAIR COVER-UP
CHECK IT OUT

YOU WILL NEED:

- Decorator fabric
- Contrasting fabric for reverse side of cover
- Measuring tape, string, or ribbon

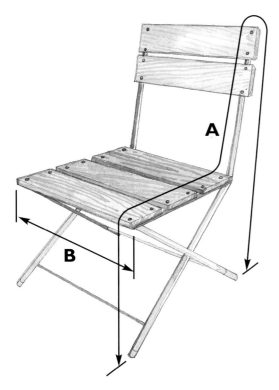

1 For the reversible cover-up measurement, measure the chair front from the floor up over the seat and chair back, then down the back to the floor (A). (Note: Run a long piece of string or ribbon over the chair and measure.)

2 Cut one cover-up piece from each fabric according to the measurement determined in step 1 plus 1" by the width of the chair (B) plus 1". Cut six ties 2" x 6".

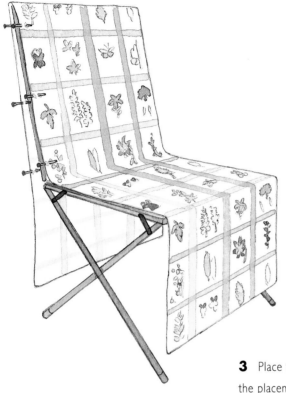

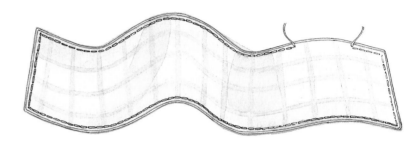

5 Stitch the cover-up pieces, right sides together, along all edges with a ¹/₂" seam allowance, leaving an opening for turning. Trim the corners, turn the cover-up right side out, and press. Stitch the opening closed.

3 Place the fabric over the chair and mark the placement of the ties along the chair back.

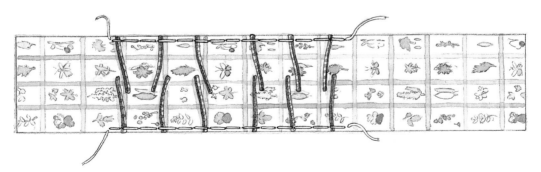

4 Make the ties as directed in step 7, Chair Skirt with Pleated Corners, page 46. Pin the ties to the fabric at the markings, keeping the ends of the ties even with the edge of the fabric. Machine-baste the ties in place.

71

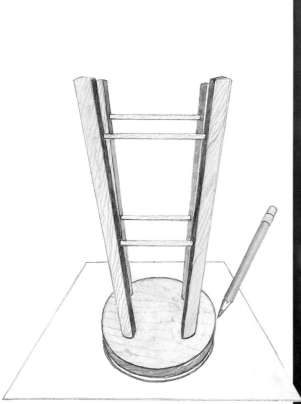

1 Place the bar stool upside down on tracing paper. Trace around the outer edge of the seat.

BAR STOOL CUSHION COVER
ADD A CUSHION

YOU WILL NEED:

- Decorator fabric
- Zipper (length equal to the diameter of the stool minus 2")
- Cording equal to twice the circumference of the stool plus 2"
- 6" of Velcro® brand Soft & Flexible SEW-ON tape
- Basting tape
- Pattern tracing paper
- Foam cushion the diameter of the bar stool by 2" thick

2 Make the pattern for the cushion top by adding $\frac{1}{2}$" around the outer edge of the seat tracing (A). Make a second pattern for the bottom of the cushion, dividing the seat tracing in half, and add $\frac{1}{2}$" seam allowance to all the edges the of pattern (B).

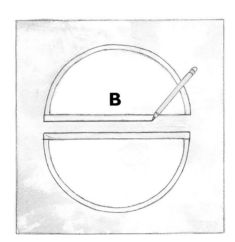

3 Cut out one cushion top piece and two cushion bottom pieces. Cut a boxing strip (the strip of fabric that runs along the side of the cushion) the circumference of the bar stool seat plus 1" by 3". Cut two strips of fabric one-half the diameter of the stool seat plus 4" by 6".

4 With right sides together, baste the cushion bottom pieces together along the straight edge and press the seam open.

5 Place a zipper along the seam, right side down, holding the zipper in place with basting tape.

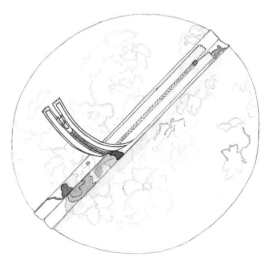

continued

73

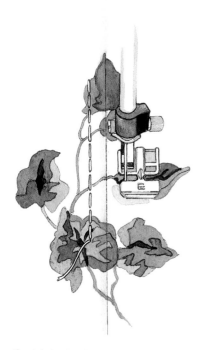

6 Stitch the zipper in place from the right side of the fabric using a zipper foot. Carefully remove the basting stitches from the seam.

7 Make piping as directed in Piping, Chapter 1. Pin the piping to the cushion top, keeping the raw edge of the piping even with the raw edge of the cushion fabric. Clip the seam allowance of the piping as needed to fit.

8 Begin stitching 2" from the cut end of the piping. Stop stitching 2" before your starting point and open out the piping. Trim the cord so it will butt up against the cord starting point.

9 Turn the raw end of the bias strip under and wrap it around the two chord ends.

10 Continue stitching. Repeat piping application on the cushion bottom.

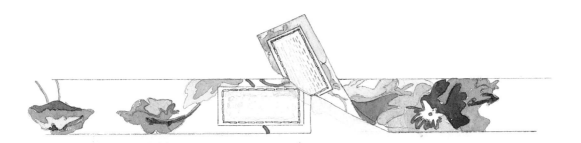

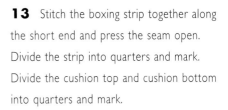

11 Stitch the straps, right sides together, along the long edge and one short edge. Trim the seams, turn right side out, and press. Sew one side of the hook and loop

tape to the front of one strap and the remaining side of the hook and loop tape to the back of the remaining strap.

12 Join the straps together at the hook and loop tape. Baste the raw edges of the straps to the cushion bottom at the sides.

13 Stitch the boxing strip together along the short end and press the seam open. Divide the strip into quarters and mark. Divide the cushion top and cushion bottom into quarters and mark.

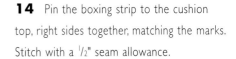

14 Pin the boxing strip to the cushion top, right sides together, matching the marks. Stitch with a $^1/_2$" seam allowance.

15 Repeat, pinning the boxing strip to the cushion bottom, being sure to open the zipper before stitching the seam. Turn the cushion right side out through the zipper opening. Insert the pillow form and zip closed.

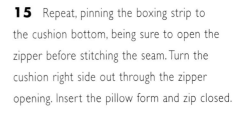

BAR STOOL SLIPCOVER
A SHEER COVER-UP

YOU WILL NEED:

- Sheer fabric
- Pattern tracing paper
- Marking pen

1 For the slipcover seat, trace around the bar stool seat as directed in Step 1, Bar Stool Cushion Cover, page 72. Add $^1/_2$" to the edge of the tracing and cut out one seat piece from the fabric. For the skirt, measure around the bottom of the stool at the base of the legs and divide by 4. Cut four skirt pieces to this measurement plus 4" by the desired skirt length plus $2^1/_2$".

2 Turn and press a 1" double-fold hem at the bottom of each skirt piece (see Hems, Chapter 1). Topstitch the hems in place.

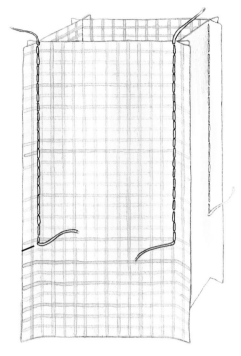

3 Stitch the skirt pieces, right sides together, along the lengthwise edges with a 1" seam allowance. End the stitching 12" from the bottom edge of the skirt. Clip the seam to the end of the stitching and press the seam open.

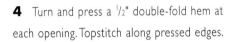

4 Turn and press a ½" double-fold hem at each opening. Topstitch along pressed edges.

5 Divide the seat cover into quarters and mark. Stitch two rows of basting along the top edge of the skirt to gather slightly. Match the skirt seams to the marks on the seat cover, right sides together, gathering the fabric as needed, and pin. Stitch using a ½" seam allowance.

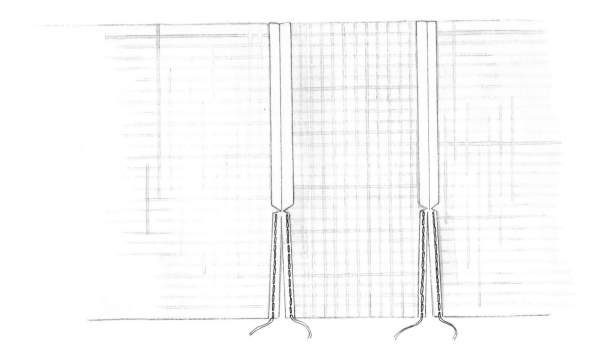

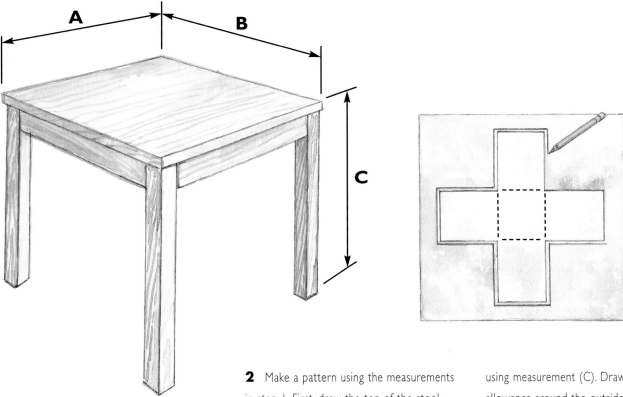

1 Measure the width (A), depth (B), and desired skirt length (C) of the stool and record the measurements.

2 Make a pattern using the measurements in step 1. First, draw the top of the stool using measurements (A) and (B). Then draw a skirt panel on each side of the stool top using measurement (C). Draw a $1/2$" seam allowance around the outside edge of the pattern.

3 Cut one stool piece from each fabric.

continued

STOOL SLIPCOVER WITH TIES
FOOTSTOOL MAGIC

YOU WILL NEED:

- Decorator fabric
- Contrasting fabric for lining
- Grommets and grommet tool
- Decorative ribbon or cord
- Pattern tracing paper
- Ruler or straight edge

4 Stitch the cover and the lining, right sides together, using a $^1/_2$" seam allowance, leaving an opening on one edge for turning. Trim the seams, clipping into the inside corners, and cut diagonally across the outside corners. Turn right side out and press. Stitch the opening closed.

5 Mark the placement for the grommets at a midpoint on each skirt edge. Insert the grommets (see Attaching Grommets, Chapter 1).

6 Place the slipcover over the stool, thread cord or ribbon through each set of grommets, and tie.

CUSHION COVER WITH RUFFLED SKIRT
FOOTSTOOL RUFFLES

YOU WILL NEED:

• Decorator fabric

• Cording equal to twice the outside
measurement of the cushion plus 4"

• 2"-3" thick foam cushion cut to the
measurement of bench or stool seat

• zipper

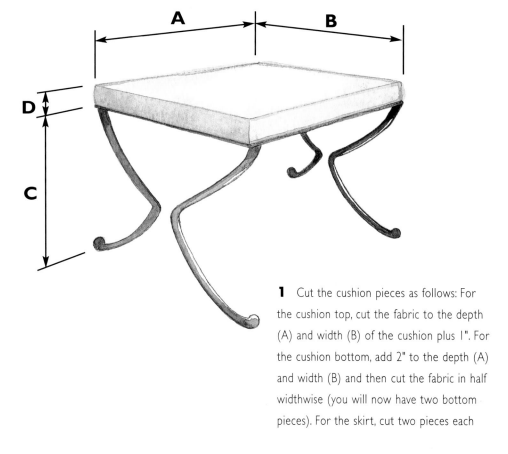

1 Cut the cushion pieces as follows: For the cushion top, cut the fabric to the depth (A) and width (B) of the cushion plus 1". For the cushion bottom, add 2" to the depth (A) and width (B) and then cut the fabric in half widthwise (you will now have two bottom pieces). For the skirt, cut two pieces each

equal to two and one-half times the width (B) of the cushion by the desired length (C) plus 2¹/₂". Cut two skirt pieces two and one-half times the depth (A) of the cushion by the desired skirt length (C) plus 2¹/₂". Cut the boxing strip (strip of fabric that runs around the side of the cushion) the measurement of all four sides of the cushion plus 1" by the height of the cushion (D) plus 1".

2 Insert the zipper as directed in the Bar Stool Cushion Cover, page 72.

3 Apply the piping as directed in the Bar Stool Cushion Cover, page 72.

4 Turn up and stitch a 1" double-fold hem on the side and bottom edges of each skirt piece. Stitch two rows of machine basting along top edge of each skirt piece for gathering.

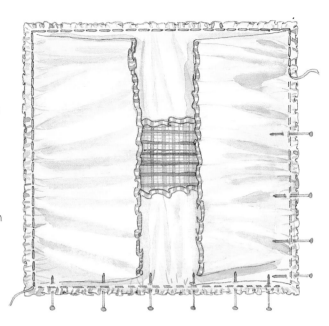

5 Pin one skirt piece to each side of the cushion bottom. Gather using the basting stitches and adjusting the gathers evenly. Stitch the skirt in place.

6 Stitch the boxing strip together along the short edge and press the seam open. Complete the cushion cover as directed in Bar Stool Cushion Cover, page 72, steps 14 through 16.

CHAPTER 4
SWEET DREAMS

Is it time to spruce up your bedroom? Slipcovers and cover-ups are the perfect solution for recycling old comforters and pillows and creating a beautifully decorated room. Duvet covers and pillow shams are simply slipcovers for your bed. Constructing these bedroom "slipcovers" couldn't be easier. A few rectangles and squares of fabric in coordinating colors and prints and a straight seam or two will have your bedroom looking decorator-perfect in no time.

CALCULATING YARDAGE FOR DUVET COVERS, COVERLETS, AND PILLOWS

DUVET COVER: To determine the finished size of the duvet cover, measure the length and width of the comforter you are covering.

COVERLET: To determine the finished size of the coverlet, measure the length of the bed plus the finished drop length for one end and the width of the bed plus two times the finished drop length.

Calculating Yardage

CUT LENGTH

A. Length of duvet or coverlet plus seam allowances

_____

CUT WIDTH

B. Width of duvet or coverlet plus seam allowances

_____ =

C. Fabric width divided by (B) = number of fabric widths required _____

CALCULATE YARDAGE

D. Cut length (A) _____ X

E. Multiply by number of widths (C) _____ =

F. Total length _____

G. Yardage required = (F) divided by 36" _____

CALCULATING ADDITIONAL YARDAGE FOR DESIGN REPEATS

H. Multiply the repeat (measure the distance between repeating designs along the selvage) by the number of fabric widths (C) needed for your project. Round to the nearest $^1/_4$-yard. _____

I. Add (H) to the yardage requirement (G)_____

For example: If the repeat is 25" and two fabric widths are required for your project, you will need an additional 40" or $1^1/_4$ yards (two x 25" = 50") rounded to the nearest $^1/_4$ yard = $1^1/_2$ yards.

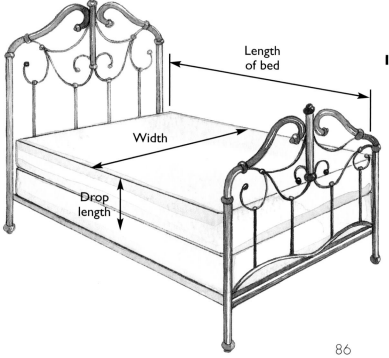

Length of bed

Width

Drop length

Measuring Pillows and Shams

Measure bed pillows and pillow forms for perfect-fitting shams and pillow covers. Very often a pillow form will measure slightly larger or smaller than the label indicates.

Measure pillows crosswise from edge to edge to determine the width (A) and from top to bottom to determine the height (B).

AVERAGE YARDAGE REQUIREMENTS FOR PILLOWS AND SHAMS

16" square—$^1/_2$ yard

18" square—$^5/_8$ yard

Standard size flanged sham—$1^3/_4$ yards

King size flanged sham—2 yards

(Add extra fabric for matching large prints)

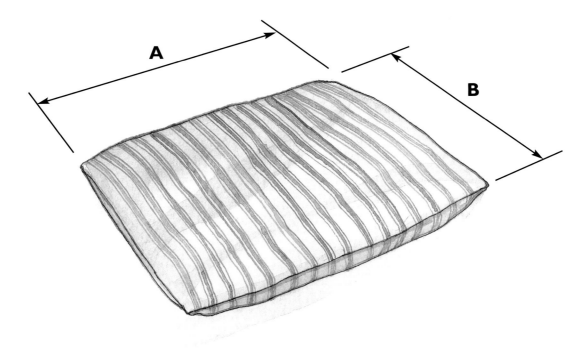

MATCHING PRINTS

Most fabrics used for your home decorating projects will require piecing to achieve the required width. When piecing fabric, prints should be perfectly matched along the seamline. Allow extra yardage for matching patterns with a distinct design and repeat.

1 Fold the side edge of the fabric under and finger-press. Lay the folded edge over the next panel of fabric and match the patterns. Pin in place. Set your sewing machine to a zigzag stitch and loosen the tension. Stitch along the fold so one swing of the needle just pierces the fold.

2 Turn the fabric to the wrong side and open out. You will see a ladder stitch formed by the stitching.

3 Using the ladder stitches as a guide, stitch the panels with right sides together. Press the seam open and remove the ladder stitch.

DUVET COVER
TROPICAL FOREST

YOU WILL NEED:

- Decorator fabric for duvet top
- Coordinating fabric for underside of duvet
- Velcro® brand Soft & Flexible
SEW-ON tape
- Decorative cording with a lip
equal to the measurement of three
sides of the duvet plus 2"

1 Measure the length and width of the duvet or comforter to be covered. Cut the fabric to the required length plus 2" by the width plus 1".

2 To piece the duvet fabric, use a full width of fabric for the center of the duvet and divide the remaining width in half, then sew to each side of the center panel. Piece the fabric according to the instructions for Matching Prints, page 88.

3 Baste the decorative cording to the side and bottom edges of the duvet cover front.

continued

90

4 Using a $1/2$" seam allowance, begin
stitching the duvet front and back, right sides
together, along the top edge, using a normal
stitch length along the outer panel and
switching to a basting stitch across the
center panel. Change back to a normal stitch
length for the remaining outer panel.

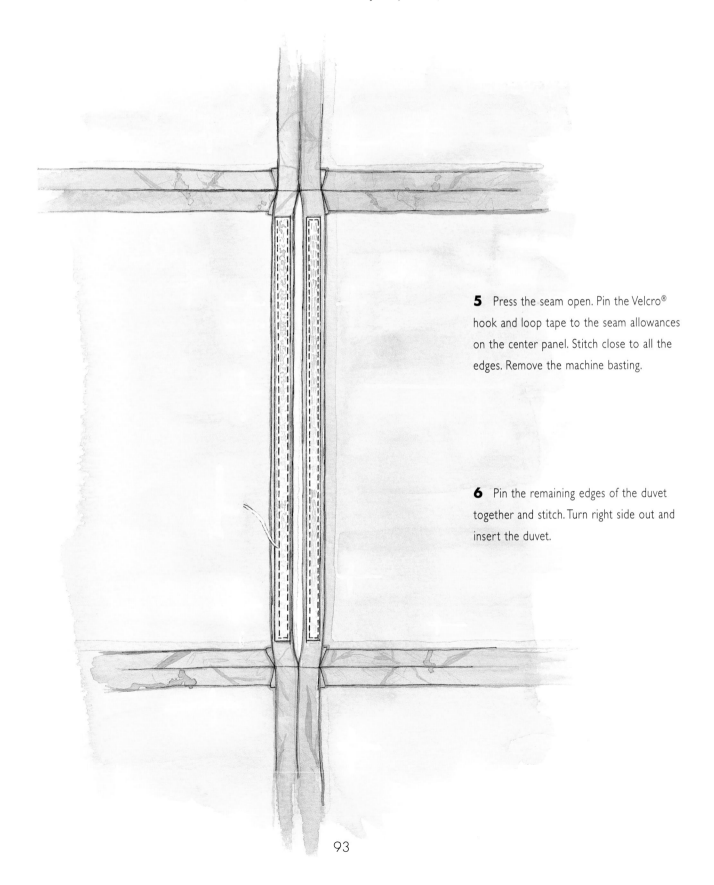

5 Press the seam open. Pin the Velcro® hook and loop tape to the seam allowances on the center panel. Stitch close to all the edges. Remove the machine basting.

6 Pin the remaining edges of the duvet together and stitch. Turn right side out and insert the duvet.

1 Cut the coverlet fabric to the required size plus 1" for seam allowances (see Calculating Yardage for Duvet Covers, Coverlets, and Pillows, page 86). The fabric will need to be pieced to reach the required coverlet width (see Matching Prints, page 88).

2 Piece the coverlet front and back as instructed in the Duvet Cover, page 90. Cover the cording for piping (see Piping, Chapter 1).

3 Baste the piping around all four sides of the coverlet front (see Bar Stool Cushion Cover, Chapter 3).

4 Stitch the coverlet front to back with right sides together, leaving an opening along the top edge for turning.

5 Turn right side out and press. Stitch the opening closed.

FRENCH COVERLET
IT'S FISHY

YOU WILL NEED:

• Decorator fabric for front of coverlet

• Contrasting fabric for back of coverlet

• Contrasting fabric for custom piping

• Cord for piping equal to all four sides of coverlet plus 3"

1 Measure the pillow to be covered. Cut the fabric the width of the pillow plus 1" by the height of the pillow plus 1" for both front and back.

2 Make a pattern for the sham flap. Draw a triangle with side (A) equal to the width of the pillow plus 1" and the length (B) equal to $^2/_3$ of the height of the pillow. Add a $^1/_2$" seam allowance to all edges. Cut two flap pieces.

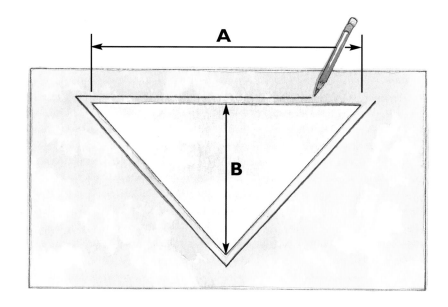

3 Using a $^1/_2$" seam allowance, stitch one flap piece to the sham back, right sides together, along the top edge of sham. Press the seam toward the flap.

continued

96

Envelope Sham
IT'S A JUNGLE

YOU WILL NEED:

- Decorator fabric for front and back of sham
- Contrasting fabric for envelope flap
- Decorative trim equal to outer edges of sham and flap
- Covered button
- Decorative tassel

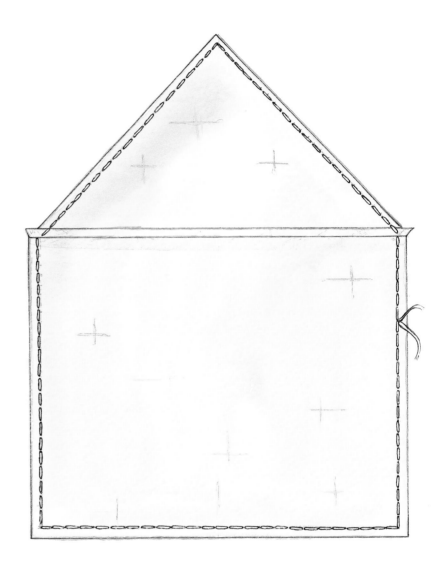

4 Turn under ¹/₂" along the top edge of the remaining sham flap piece and press. Turn under ¹/₂" along the sham front piece and topstitch the sham front only.

5 With rights sides together, stitch the sham front and the flap facing pieces to the flap and back along the outer edges.

6 Trim the corners and seams. Turn the sham and flap right side out and slipstitch the flap facing along the pressed edge.

7 Pin the trim to the right side of the sham front along the two sides and bottom edges. Stitch in place. Repeat along the edge of the sham flap.

8 Cover a button according to the manufacturer's directions. Stitch the button to the point of the sham flap. Tie the tassel around the button.

FLANGED SHAM
BAMBOO HIGHLIGHTS

YOU WILL NEED:

• Decorator fabric
• Decorative cord with lip equal to the
measurement of all sides of the sham plus 2"

1 For the sham front, cut the fabric the
width of the pillow plus 5" by the height of
the pillow plus 5". For the sham back, cut the
fabric the width of the pillow plus 2" by the
height of the pillow plus 5". For the back
overlap, cut a piece of fabric 12" wide by the
height of the pillow plus 5".

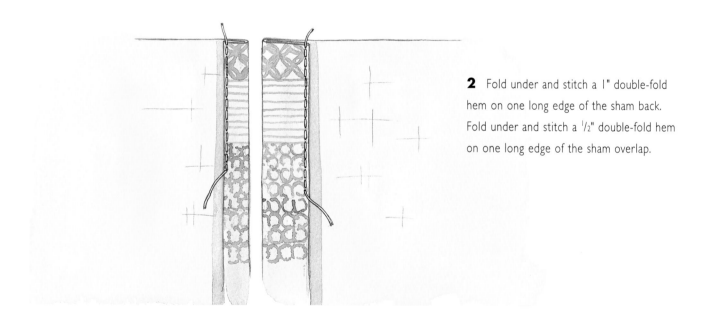

2 Fold under and stitch a 1" double-fold
hem on one long edge of the sham back.
Fold under and stitch a $\frac{1}{2}$" double-fold hem
on one long edge of the sham overlap.

100

3 Baste the cord to the right side of the sham front keeping the edge of the cord even with the raw edge of the sham. Begin sewing 2" from the end of the cord and stop sewing 2" from your starting point.

continued

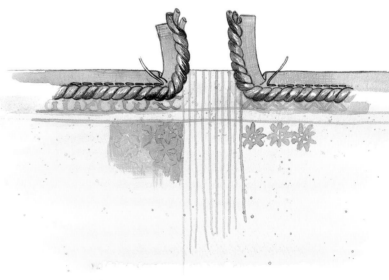

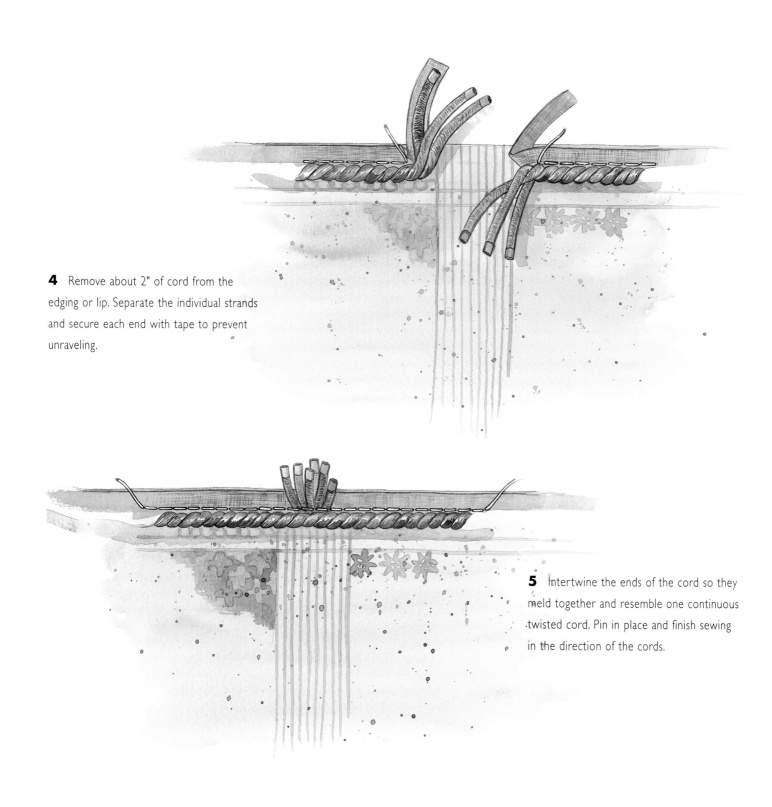

4 Remove about 2" of cord from the edging or lip. Separate the individual strands and secure each end with tape to prevent unraveling.

5 Intertwine the ends of the cord so they meld together and resemble one continuous twisted cord. Pin in place and finish sewing in the direction of the cords.

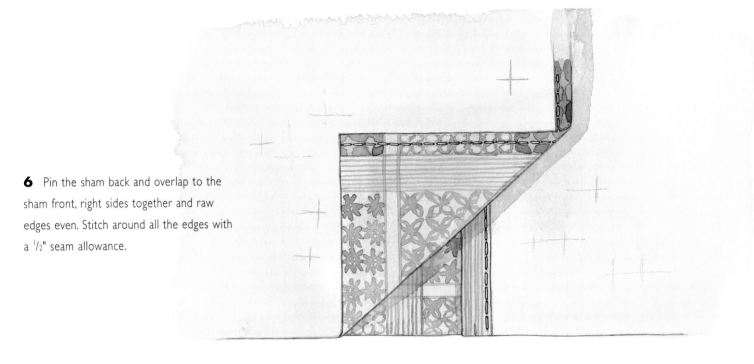

6 Pin the sham back and overlap to the sham front, right sides together and raw edges even. Stitch around all the edges with a $\frac{1}{2}$" seam allowance.

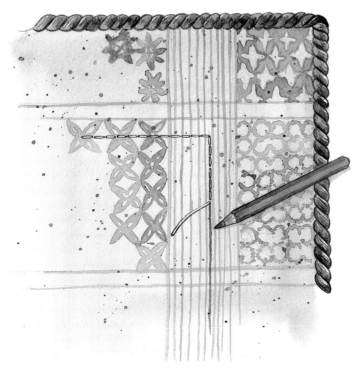

7 Turn the sham right side out and press. Measure in 2" from the finished edge and draw a stitching line. Pin through all the layers to hold the fabric pieces in place. Stitch along the marked line.

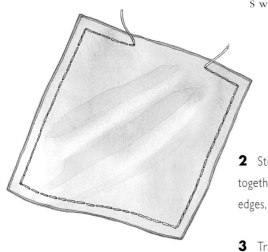

2 Stitch the inside pillow pieces, right sides together, with a $1/2$" seam allowance along all edges, leaving an opening for turning.

3 Trim the corners and turn right side out. Insert the pillow form and slipstitch the opening closed.

1 For the inside pillow, measure the pillow form and cut two pieces of fabric 1" larger than the pillow form. For the cover-up, cut two pieces of fabric 1" larger than the pillow form, cut six ties 1" wide by 7" long, and cut two facing pieces the height of the pillow plus 1" by $4^{1}/2$".

4 Sew the cover-up, right sides together, along the top and bottom edges and one side edge. Clip the corners and turn right side out.

5 Make the ties as directed in Chair Back Cover-up with Ties, Chapter 3.

7 Stitch the facing pieces, right sides together, along the short edges with a $1/2$" seam allowance. Press the seams flat. Finish one edge of the facing with a serger or use a narrow hem.

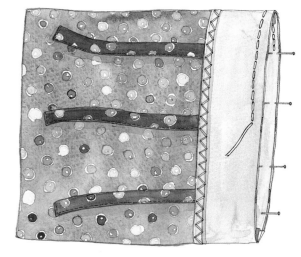

8 Pin the facing over the open end of the pillow cover-up, matching the seams. Stitch in place with a $1/2$" seam allowance. Press the facing to the inside. Insert the pillow and tie.

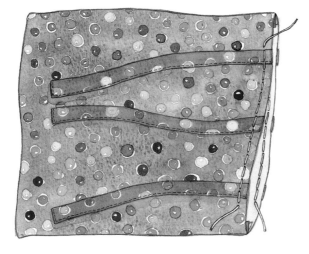

6 Baste the ties to the right side of the open edge of the cover-up, placing three ties on the front of the cover-up and three ties on the back.

SIMPLE PILLOW WITH TIE-ON COVER-UP
TIE IT ON

YOU WILL NEED:

• Decorator fabric for inside pillow

• Contrasting fabric for tie-on cover-up

BUTTON-ON PILLOW SLIPCOVER
BUTTON IT UP

YOU WILL NEED:

- Decorator fabric
- Covered buttons

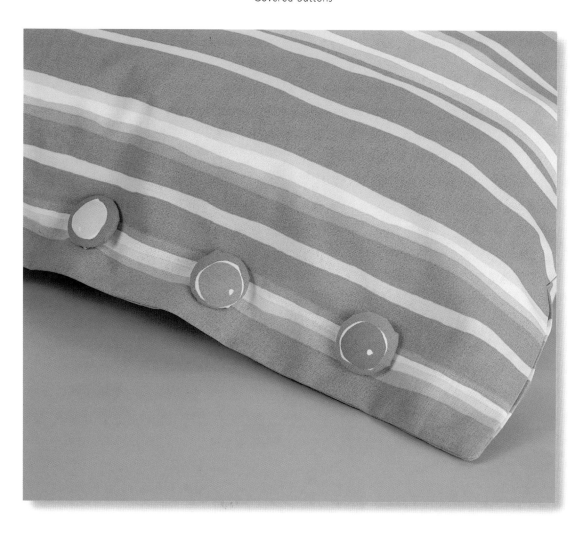

1 Measure the pillow form and cut two pieces of fabric the height of the pillow plus 1" by the width of the pillow plus 12".

2 Stitch the pillow cover with right sides together and $1/2$" seam allowance along three edges.

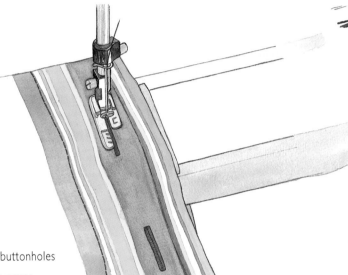

3 Finish the raw edge of the open end of the pillow cover with a serger or use a narrow hem. Turn in the edge 3" around the opening and topstitch in place.

4 Mark the placement for the buttonholes along the open end of the pillow cover. Stitch each buttonhole.

5 Mark the placement of the buttons on the inside edge of the pillow cover. Stitch the buttons at the markings.

6 Insert the pillow and button the cover-up.

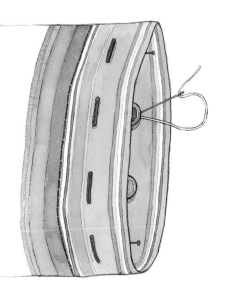

1 Measure your pillow form. Cut the fabric to twice the width of the pillow plus 1" by the height of the pillow plus 12".

2 Finish one long edge of the fabric with a serger or narrow hem. Fold the fabric in half crosswise. Stitch along the side and bottom edges with a ¹/₂" seam allowance.

SACK PILLOW COVER
BAG IT!

YOU WILL NEED:

- Decorator fabric
- $^3/_4$ of a yard of coordinating ribbon

3 Turn the top edge down 6" to the wrong side. Stitch in place close to the finished edge and turn right side out.

4 Insert the pillow into the sack. Tie the ribbon around the top of the pillow form.

CHAPTER 5

HIDE AND SEEK

Slipcovers can not only update a worn or out-of-date piece of furniture, but they can also solve storage problems in a cost-effective, decorative way.

Transform any room with decorative fabric cover-ups to match the curtains or other furniture pieces. Mix or match prints, introduce a new color, or add texture to the surroundings.

VANITY TABLE SKIRT
FIT FOR A PRINCESS

YOU WILL NEED:

- Tulle or netting (for two skirt layers)
- Lightweight fabric for underskirt
- Velcro® brand Half & Half™ tape
- Scraps of decorative fabric for top band of skirt
- Silk flowers in assorted sizes
- Low-heat glue gun

1 Cut the fabric as follows: For the top band, cut a strip of fabric 7" wide by the outside measurement of the vanity tabletop plus 1". For the skirt, cut two pieces of tulle the length of the table less 2½" by three times the outside measurement of the table-top. Cut one piece of lining the length of the table by three times the outside measurement of the table. Piece the lining as needed.

2 Press the skirt band in half lengthwise, wrong sides together, and open out flat. Pin the sew-on side of the hook and loop tape to the right side of the skirt band. Place the tape about ¼" from the center fold and stitch in place along the top and bottom edges.

3 Turn under ½" and press along the long edge of the skirt band on the opposite side from the hook and loop tape.

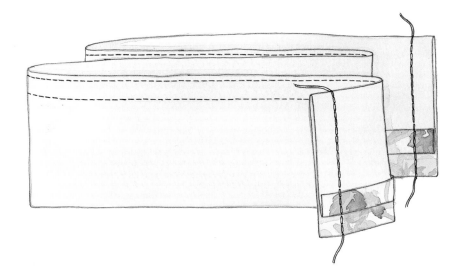

4 Fold the band, right sides together, along the fold line. Stitch the ends of the band with a $1/2$" seam allowance. Trim the corners diagonally and turn right side out; press.

5 Turn under and stitch a 1" double-fold hem along the bottom edge of the skirt lining. Stitch a narrow hem on the side edges of the skirt lining (see Hems, Chapter 1).

continued

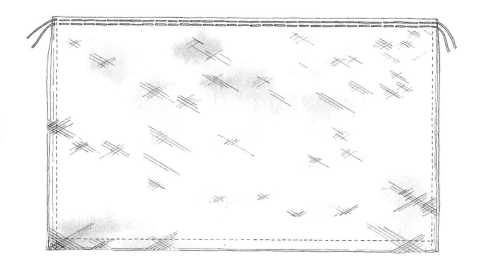

6 Layer the tulle skirt pieces and the lining, with the lining on the bottom, and stitch two rows of machine basting through all layers along the top edge of skirt.

7 Pin the right side of the band to the wrong side of the skirt with the raw edges even. Pull up on the basting stitches to evenly gather the skirt to the band. Stitch with a $1/2$" seam allowance. Press the seam allowance toward the skirt band.

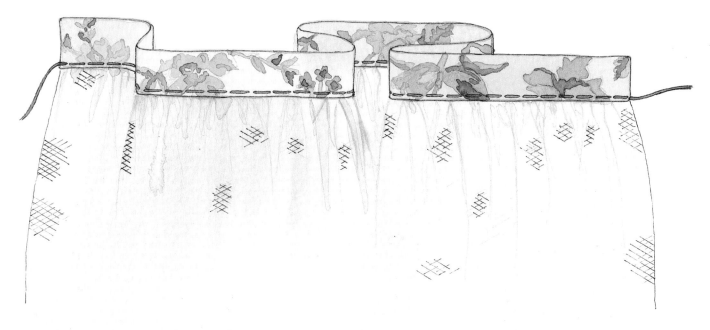

8 Pin the folded edge of the band over the skirt seam. The seam allowance will be "sandwiched" in the band. Topstitch close to the fold.

9 Clip small flowers from the stems and arrange as desired on the skirt. Secure in place with the glue gun.

10 Adhere the remaining side of the hook and loop tape to the outer edge of the vanity table. Attach the skirt to the table.

ROMAN SHADE FOR BOOKCASE
SURPRISE BEHIND

YOU WILL NEED:

- Decorator fabric
- Lining fabric
- Ring tape
- Nylon cording
- Marking pen
- White crafts glue
- $1/2$" wooden dowel—I" shorter than the finished width of your shade
- Velcro® brand Half & Half™ tape
- Cleat

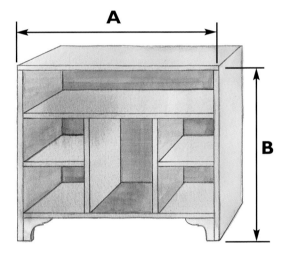

A

B

3/4"

3/4"

1 Measure the width (A) and the height (B) of the bookcase. Cut the fabric and lining to the width plus 1" by the height plus $2^{1}/_{2}$".

2 Stitch the sew-on side of the hook and loop tape to the right side of the top edge of the lining. The top edge of the hook and loop tape should be $^{3}/_{4}$" from the top and side edges of the fabric.

continued

117

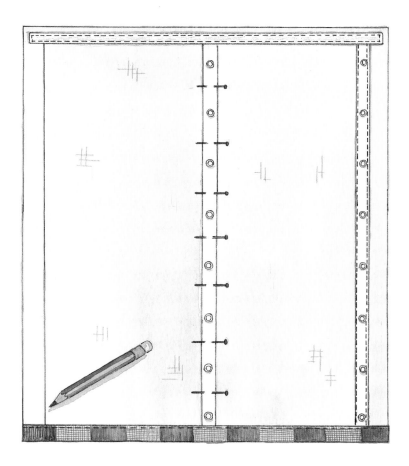

3 Stitch the lining and the fabric, right sides together, along the side and top edges with a ¹/₂" seam allowance. Turn right side out and press.

4 Turn up and stitch a 1" double-fold hem on the bottom edge of the shade (see Hems, Chapter 1).

5 Place the shade on a table, lining side up. Mark a vertical line down the center of the shade. Mark two additional lines 1" from each side edge of the shade. Pin the ring tape in place over the marked lines and stitch close to the edge of the tape. Stitch both sides of the ring tape from the bottom to the top to prevent puckering. (Note: The rings on each row of tape must be even horizontally with each other.)

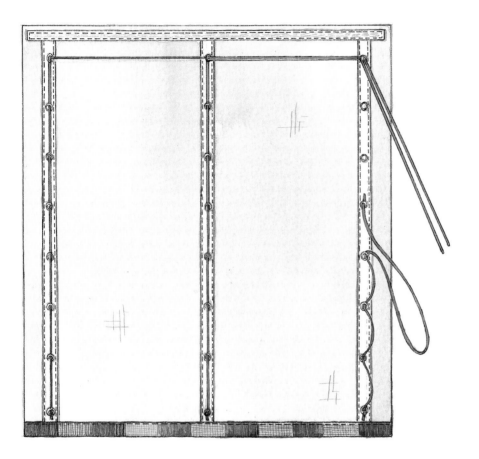

6 Cut three cords one and one-half times the length of the shade plus the width of the shade. Tie a cord to the bottom ring on each strip of ring tape. Place a drop of white glue on the knot to secure. Run the cord up through the rings and across the top of the shade so all of the cords end up on the same edge of the shade.

7 Adhere the remaining side of the hook and loop tape to the top edge of the bookcase. Attach a cleat along the inside edge of the bookcase on the same side as the cords.

8 Insert a dowel into bottom edge of the shade through the hem. Attach the shade to the bookcase with the hook and loop tape. Pull the cords to raise the shade, adjusting so the shade is even. Tie the cords together and trim to an even length. To keep the shade in a raised position, wrap the cords around the cleat.

FILING CABINET COVER-UP
KEEP IT ORGANIZED

YOU WILL NEED:

- Decorator fabric
- Velcro® brand Soft & Flexible SEW-ON tape

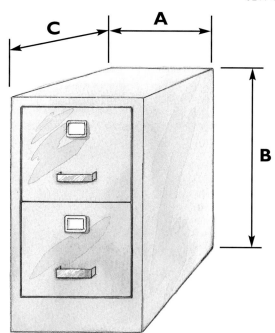

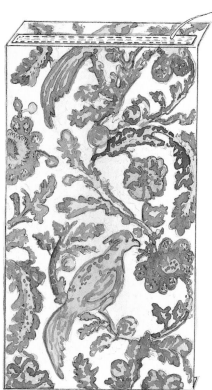

1 Measure each side of your file cabinet and record the measurements. Cut the fabric as follows: For the back, cut one piece of fabric the width of the cabinet (A) plus 1" by the height of the cabinet (B) plus 1½". For the sides, cut two pieces of fabric the depth (C) plus 2½" by the height (B) plus 1½". For the top, cut one piece of fabric the width of the top (A) plus 1" by the depth of the top (C) plus 2". For the front, cut one piece of fabric the height (B) of the front plus 3" by the width (A) of the front plus 4".

2 Finish the side and top edges of the slipcover front with a serger or narrow hem so the edges don't fray. On the bottom edge of the front, turn under and topstitch a ½" double-fold hem (see Hems, Chapter 1).

3 Turn under and stitch a 2" blind hem on each side edge of the front panel (see Hems, Chapter 1).

4 Turn under a 1½" hem on the top edge and press. Open out the hem and stitch one side of the hook and loop tape to the top hem ¼" from the pressed fold. Stitch the hem in place using a blind hem stitch.

5 Stitch the back to the sides along the back edges, right sides together, with a ½" seam allowance. Press the seams open.

continued

120

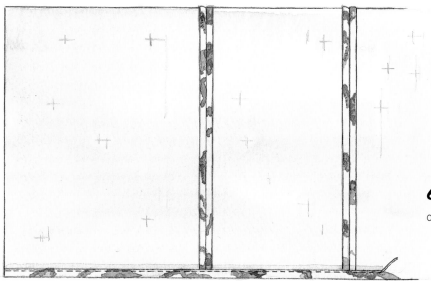

6 Turn up and stitch a ¹/₂" double-fold hem on the bottom edge of the back and sides.

7 Finish the front edge of the slipcover sides with a serger or turn under ¹/₄" and stitch in place. Press under 2" to the wrong side of the front side edges. Machine-baste along the top edge.

8 Finish the front edge of the slipcover top. Turn under 1 ¹/₂" along the finished edge and press. Open out the fabric and stitch the remaining side of the hook and loop tape ¹/₄" from the fold.

9 Pin the sides and back of the slipcover to the top of the slipcover, right sides together. Match the seams to the back corners of the top with the front edges of the side even with the fold. Stitch with a $1/2$" seam allowance. Turn right side out.

10 Slipstitch the remaining front edges of the slipcover top to the sides of the slipcover.

11 Place the slipcover over the file cabinet. Attach the slipcover front along the hook and loop tape strip.

1 Measure the table as follows: Measure
the width (A) and depth (B) of the tabletop;
measure around the outer edge of the two
short sides and one long side of table (C);
and measure the height of the table (D).

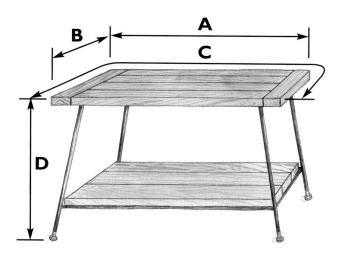

2 Cut the slipcover pieces as follows: Cut
the slipcover top 1" larger than the measurement of the tabletop. Cut the slipcover skirt
the measurement of (C) plus one-half the
long side of the table (A) plus 52" by the
height of the table plus 4½". Your fabric may
need to be pieced (see Matching Prints,
Chapter 4). Cut the removable panel one-
half the measurement of the long side of the
table (A) plus 8" by the height of the table
plus 5". Cut the front panel facing one-half
the width of the long side of the table (A)
plus 3" by 4" wide.

3 Make piping as directed in Chapter 1.
Baste the piping to the slipcover top (see
Bar Stool Cushion Cover, Chapter 3).

124

SOFA TABLE SLIPCOVER
CHINA HIDEAWAY

YOU WILL NEED:

• Velcro® brand Soft & Flexible SEW-ON tape

• Cording equal to the measurement of all sides of the tabletop plus 4"

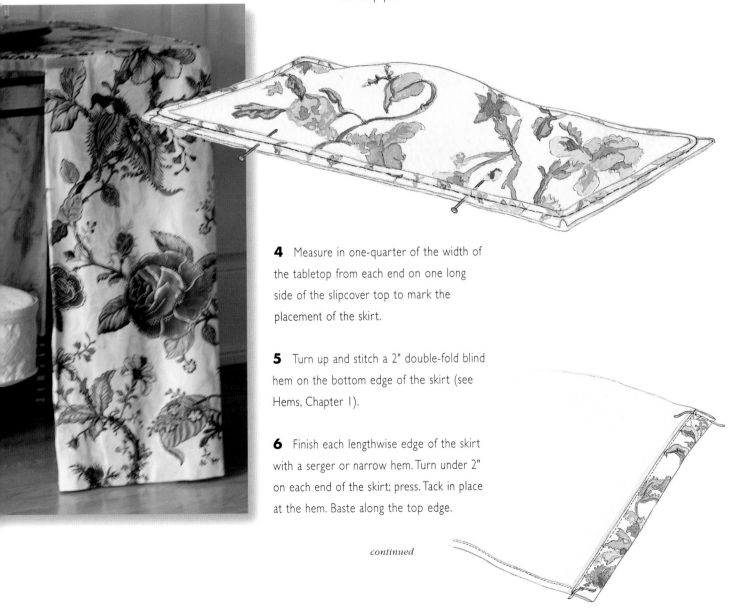

4 Measure in one-quarter of the width of the tabletop from each end on one long side of the slipcover top to mark the placement of the skirt.

5 Turn up and stitch a 2" double-fold blind hem on the bottom edge of the skirt (see Hems, Chapter 1).

6 Finish each lengthwise edge of the skirt with a serger or narrow hem. Turn under 2" on each end of the skirt; press. Tack in place at the hem. Baste along the top edge.

continued

125

7 To make the front corner pleats in the skirt, begin at the right front edge of skirt. Measure along the top of the skirt one-quarter of the width of the table plus 6" and mark. (For example, if the table is 40" wide, you will measure over 46" and make a mark.) Repeat this process with the left front edge of the skirt. This will be the center of the pleat. Make a pleat as directed in Chair Skirt with Pleated Corners, Chapter 3.

8 To mark the location of the remaining pleats, measure from the center of each completed pleat, the depth of the tabletop plus 6", and mark. This will be the center point for the remaining pleats. Complete the pleats as in step 7.

9 With right sides together, pin the skirt to the slipcover top, matching the front edges of the skirt with the marks on the top front and matching each pleat to a corner of the top piece. Fold the facing in half length-wise, wrong sides together, and press. Pin along the center front of the slipcover top. Baste in place.

10 Stitch the skirt to the slipcover top around all four edges.

11 Turn up and stitch a 2" double-fold blind hem on the bottom edge of the removable panel. Finish the side and top edges of the removable panel with a serger or narrow hem.

12 Turn under 2" along each side edge of the panel and press. Slipstitch at the hem.

13 Stitch one side of the hook and loop tape to the right side of the panel, $^{1}/_{2}$" from the top edge.

14 Turn under 1" along the top edge of the panel and press. Topstitch or blind hem in place.

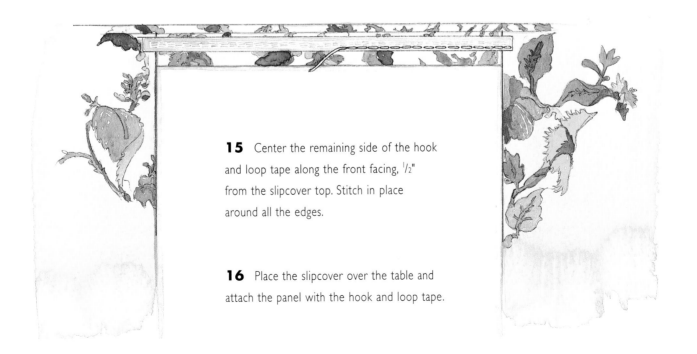

15 Center the remaining side of the hook and loop tape along the front facing, $^{1}/_{2}$" from the slipcover top. Stitch in place around all the edges.

16 Place the slipcover over the table and attach the panel with the hook and loop tape.

STORAGE SHELF SLIPCOVER
IT'S FOR KIDS

YOU WILL NEED:

- Decorator fabric for body of slipcover
- Contrasting fabric for top and front panel of slipcover
- Velcro® brand Soft & Flexible SEW-ON tape

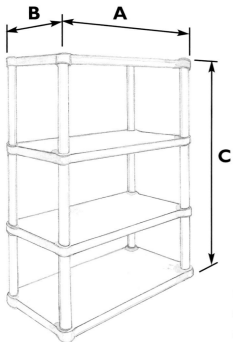

1 Measure the shelf and cut the fabric as follows: For the slipcover top, cut the fabric the width (A) and depth (B) of the shelves plus 1". For the scalloped flap, cut two pieces of fabric the width of the shelves (A) plus 1" by 13". For the slipcover back, cut the fabric the width (A) of the shelves plus 1" by the height of the shelves (C) plus 1½". For the sides, cut two pieces of fabric, the depth of the shelves (B) plus 1" by the height of the shelves (C) plus 1½". For the front, cut two

pieces of fabric the width of the shelves minus 2" by the height of the shelves plus 2"; mark one piece left front and one piece right front. For the front bands, cut two pieces of fabric 7" wide by the height of the shelves plus 1½".

2 Cut a strip of hook and loop tape the width of the shelf minus 2". On the right side of one flap piece, stitch one side of hook and loop tape ¾" from the top edge of the flap and 1" from each side edge of the flap.

3 Divide the remaining side of the hook and loop tape in half and stitch one piece to the right and left front pieces, 1½" from the top edges.

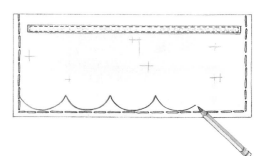

4 Baste the two top flap pieces, right sides together, along the two sides and bottom edge. Trace a scallop along the bottom edge, just above the basting line.

continued

5 Using a normal stitch length, stitch along the marked scalloped and the two side edges. Trim the seam and clip the curves.

6 Turn right side out and press. Machine-baste along the top edge of the flap.

7 With right sides together, pin the flap to the slipcover top. Stitch in place with a ¹/₂" seam allowance. (Note: The Velcro® will be on the wrong side or back of the flap.)

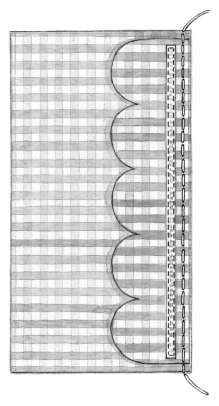

8 Fold the front bands in half lengthwise, wrongs side together, and press. Open out the bands.

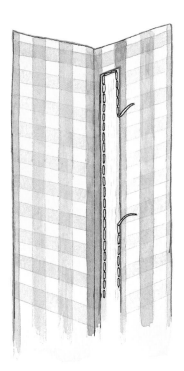

9 Cut a strip of hook and loop tape the length of the bands minus 3". Center one side of the hook and loop tape to the right of the fold on each band piece and stitch around all the edges.

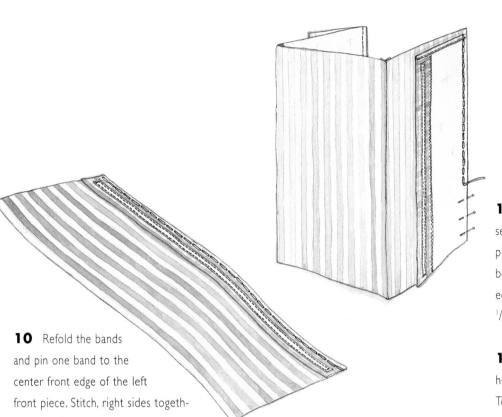

10 Refold the bands and pin one band to the center front edge of the left front piece. Stitch, right sides together, with a $1/2$" seam allowance. Finish the seam with a serger or zigzag stitch.

11 Pin the remaining band to the center front edge of the right front piece with the remaining tape to the right side. Stitch with a $1/2$" seam allowance. Finish the seam with a serger or zigzag stitch.

12 Turn under and press a $1/2$" double-fold hem on the top edge of the slipcover front pieces. Topstitch in place.

13 With right sides together, using a $1/2$" seam allowance, stitch the slipcover back to the slipcover sides.

14 With right sides together, using a $1/2$" seam allowance, stitch the slipcover front pieces to the slipcover sides. Match the bottom edge of the front with the bottom edge of the side. The front pieces will end $1/2$" below the top edge of the sides.

15 Turn under and press a $1/2$" double-fold hem on the bottom edge of the slipcover. Topstitch in place.

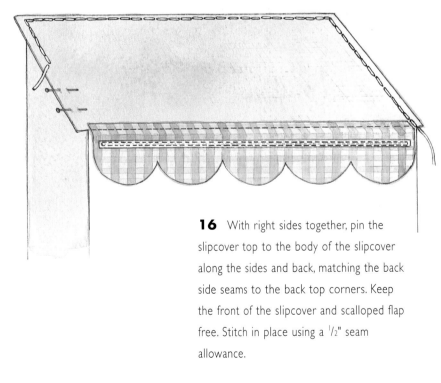

16 With right sides together, pin the slipcover top to the body of the slipcover along the sides and back, matching the back side seams to the back top corners. Keep the front of the slipcover and scalloped flap free. Stitch in place using a $1/2$" seam allowance.

17 Place the slipcover over the shelves and close.

CHAPTER 6

SPECIAL EMBELLISHMENTS

Adding extra decorative details to a slipcover can change the ordinary into the sublime. A simple rubber stamp and a bit of paint makes a plain tablecloth into one that is perfectly themed for a holiday party. For something more elaborate, add an embroidered monogram or motif. Try trimming the hems of table toppers and chair skirts with matching ribbons for a completely coordinated look. With a bit of imagination and the techniques that follow, you are sure to create unique cover-ups for every occasion.

STAMPING

Rubber stamps are available in a wide range of motifs and sizes.
Embellish a project with holiday-themed stamps, seasonal motifs, or a favorite
animal or flower. Stamping is a quick-and-easy no-sew method for adding
a decorative embellishment to your fabric.

1 Using acrylic or fabric paint, dab or "load" the stamp with your desired color. (Note: The stamp shown is loaded with different colors to give you an idea of how to use different colors on the same motif.)

2 Turn the stamp over, press evenly on the fabric, and then carefully remove the stamp. Repeat the process wherever a motif is desired. Add additional details with a paintbrush.

1 Determine the desired location on your fabric for the stencil motif. Secure the stencil with a small piece of tape on each side. Dip the brush into the paint, then blot the brush on a scrap fabric or paper towel to remove any excess paint. Using a dabbing motion, paint in the desired area of the stencil. Repeat the process filling in the remaining areas of the stencil with other colors.

2 Allow the paint to dry for a few minutes before removing the stencil. Carefully move the stencil to the next location, making sure not to smear the paint particularly if you are overlapping or joining designs. Tape the edges and continue painting.

STENCILLING

Like stamping, stencils are a great way to add a painted embellishment to a project. Stencils are available as single motifs or as borders, which are great for adding a decorative edging on long lengths of fabric. When stencilling, you will need acrylic or fabric paints, a stencil brush, and some masking tape to hold the stencil securely in place when painting.

EMBROIDERY

Sewing machines with professional embroidery capabilities offer an
endless array of design options for home decorating projects. From monograms
and animal motifs to holiday and sporting designs, the possibilities are endless.
You can even design your own embroideries using your home computer.

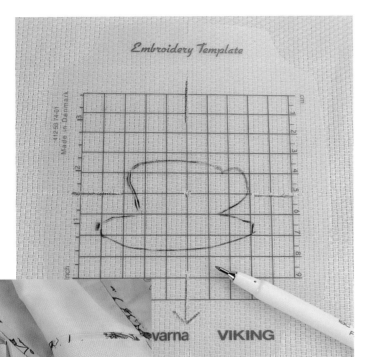

2 After selecting your motif, stitch a sample motif on a scrap of fabric. Trace the outline of the motif on the embroidery template. (Note: A template comes with the machine and is designed to work in tandem with the embroidery hoop for accurate placement.) Place the template over your fabric, positioning the embroidery outline where you would like the finished embroidery to be stitched. Using a water-soluble marker, mark the top, bottom, and sides on the fabric for hoop placement.

3 Place a piece of tear-away stabilizer underneath the fabric. Place the fabric and the stabilizer in the embroidery hoop, lining up the marks on the hoop with the marks on the fabric. Attach the hoop to the embroidery unit and begin stitching.

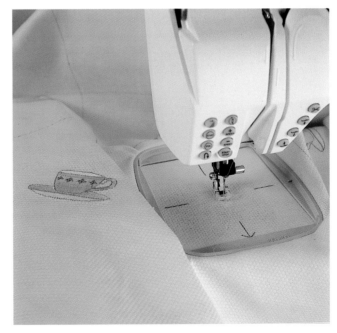

1 While each embroidery sewing machine is different, they all operate essentially the same way. The main bed of the sewing machine is removed and replaced with a complete embroidery unit. A disc or card, which has stored embroidery motifs on it, is inserted into a slot in the machine. With the touch of a button your design is sewn, stopping as each portion of the design is completed, allowing you to change thread colors for each section.

1 Before stitching the ribbon or trim in place, mark the desired location using a ruler and marking pen. Secure the ribbon or trim over the marked lines using a glue stick or basting tape.

2 Stitch the ribbon or trim in place close to the edge using an edge-stitch foot.

RIBBON AND FLAT TRIMS

Ribbon and many flat trims are available in a variety of widths, fabrics, textures, and designs. From velvets and satin, to silk or grosgrain, there is a ribbon or trim available for every decorating style. Use one or more ribbons or trims to accent a hem or create a design on a pillow for a creative touch.

LAMINATING

Laminated fabrics are great for outdoor use or when designing projects that you may
want to childproof such as kitchen tablecloths or place mats.

1 Following the manufacturer's instructions, remove the paper backing from the clear laminate. (Note: Clear laminate is available in a shiny or dull finish.)

2 Place the sticky side of the laminate on the right side of the fabric. Cover with the paper backing and press in place.

RESOURCES

Pamela Hastings

is a freelance author, spokesperson, and consultant who has been in the home sewing business for nearly 20 years. As spokesperson for Velcro USA and Waverly, she is a frequent guest on decorating and home improvement shows, such as *Interior Motives* and *Decorating with Style.* Pam also works closely with Viking Sewing Machines Inc., developing projects for home decorating publications, including *Woman's Day Specials, Better Homes and Gardens,* and *Home Magazine.*

Pam is also the author of the Sterling/Sewing Information Resources books *Creative Projects for Computerized Machines* and *Sewing Shortcuts,* and co-author of *Serger Shortcuts.*

Pam resides in Wall, New Jersey, with her husband Geof, sons Christopher and Connor, and Claudia Anne.

Sewing Equipment and Accessories:
Viking Sewing Machines Inc.
31000 Viking Parkway
Westlake, OH 44145
(800) 358-0001
www.husqvarnaviking.com

Fabric:
Coverlet and throw pillows: Laura Ashley

All other fabric:
Waverly
79 Madison Ave
NY, NY 10016
(800) 988-7775
www.waverly.com

Trims:
Conso
(800) 845-2431
www.conso.com

Rubber Stamps:
Rubber Stamp Stampede
P.O. Box 246
Berkley, CA 94701
(800) 632-8386

Pillow Forms:
Fairfield Processing
88 Rose Hill Rd.
Danbury, CT 06813
(800) 980-8000

Hook and Loop Tape:
Velcro® brand Half & Half™ tape
Velcro® brand Soft & Flexible SEW-ON tape
Velcro USA Inc.
6420 East Broadway Blvd. – Suite B-300
Tucson, AZ 85710
www.velcro.com

METRIC EQUIVALENTS

Inches to Millimeters and Centimeters
MM - millimeters   CM - centimeters

Inches	MM	CM	Inches	CM	Inches	CM
1/8	3	0.3	9	22.9	30	76.2
1/4	6	0.6	10	25.4	31	78.7
3/8	10	1.0	11	27.9	32	81.3
1/2	13	1.3	12	30.5	33	83.8
5/8	16	1.6	13	33.0	34	86.4
3/4	19	1.9	14	35.6	35	88.9
7/8	22	2.2	15	38.1	36	91.4
1	25	2.5	16	40.6	37	94.0
1 1/4	32	3.2	17	43.2	38	96.5
1 1/2	38	3.8	18	45.7	39	99.1
1 3/4	44	4.4	19	48.3	40	101.6
2	51	5.1	20	50.8	41	104.1
2 1/2	64	6.4	21	53.3	42	106.7
3	76	7.6	22	55.9	43	109.2
3 1/2	89	8.9	23	58.4	44	111.8
4	102	10.2	24	61.0	45	114.3
4 1/2	114	11.4	25	63.5	46	116.8
5	127	12.7	26	66.0	47	119.4
6	152	15.2	27	68.6	48	121.9
7	178	17.8	28	71.1	49	124.5
8	203	20.3	29	73.7	50	127.0

METRIC CONVERSION CHART

Yards		Inches	Meters	Yards	Inches
1/8	4.5	0.11	1 1/8	40.5	1.03
1/4	9	0.23	1 1/4	45	1.14
3/8	13.5	0.34	1 3/8	49.5	1.26
1/2	18	0.46	1 1/2	54	1.37
5/8	22.5	0.57	1 5/8	58.5	1.49
3/4	27	0.69	1 3/4	63	1.60
7/8	31.5	0.80	1 7/8	67.5	1.71
1	36	0.91	2	72	1.83

INDEX

INDEX

INDEX